An Alastair Reid Reader

The Bread Loaf Series of Contemporary Writers

ALASTAIR REID

An Alastair Reid
READER

SELECTED

PROSE AND POETRY

Middlebury College Press
Published by University Press of New England
Hanover and London

MIDDLEBURY COLLEGE PRESS
Published by University Press of New England,
Hanover, NH 03755
© 1994 by Alastair Reid
Acknowledgments appear on page 243
Printed in the United States of America   5   4   3   2   1

CIP data appear at the end of the book

for Leslie,

C.M.

regocijante

Contents

Contents

WORDINGS

REVIEWS, ETC.

TRANSLATION

viii

A Bread Loaf Contemporary

A T   A   T I M E   when the literary world is increasingly dominated by commercial formulas and concentrated financial power, there is a clear need to restore the simple pleasures of reading: the experience of opening a book by an author you know and being delighted by a completely new dimension of her or his art, the joy of seeing an author break free of any formula to reveal the power of the well-written word. The best writing, many authors affirm, comes as a gift; the best reading comes when the author passes that gift to the reader, a gift the author could imagine only by taking risks in a variety of genres including short stories, poetry, and essays.

As editors of The Bread Loaf Series of Contemporary Writers we subscribe to no single viewpoint. Our singular goal is to publish writing that moves the reader: by the beauty and lucidity of its language, by its underlying argument, by its force of vision. These values are celebrated each summer at the Writers' Conference on Bread Loaf Mountain in Vermont and in each of these books.

We offer you the Bread Loaf Contemporary Writers series and the treasures with which these authors have surprised us.

Robert Pack
Jay Parini

PROSE

Writing is the most portable of occupations, and since it has been my livelihood from the fifties on, I have taken full advantage of this portability and its accompanying freedom to live in a number of different countries, contexts, and languages, which in turn have intruded themselves into much of what I have written.

Living in different places means growing separate selves, learning other languages and ways of being, and looking at the world from different vantage points, without ever quite belonging to any of them. The state of being a foreigner wherever I am has become second nature to me. It is a condition that sharpens the eye and ear, that keeps awareness on its toes, and that takes nothing for granted. It means also that wherever I am, the ghosts of other places and other lives are hovering close.

Inevitably, my various preoccupations show up in this collection: with language and languages, with human oddness and eccentricity, with villages and the agrarian round, and with what geographers call "land–life relations." I have written too in many different modes. I began as a poet, and then, through a long association with The New Yorker, I wrote a variety of things for that magazine—essays, reviews, stories, chronicles from different countries, and articles on miscellaneous subjects, besides poems and translations. I was drawn to translation through my friendships with many Latin American writers and my enthusiasm for their writings. As one of them once wrote to me: "The best thing about literature is the friends it brings you."

The one constant in my shifting existence has been the island of my writing table.

Digging Up Scotland

I HAVE A FRIEND in Scotland, a painter, who still lives in the fishing town he was born in, grew up in, went to school in, was married in, raised his children in, works in, and clearly intends to die in. I look on him with uncomprehending awe, for although I had much the same origins that he had, born and sprouting in rural Scotland, close to the sea, living more by the agrarian round than by outside time, I had in my head from an early age the firm notion of leaving, long before I knew why or how. Even less did I realize then that I would come to restless rest in a whole slew of places, countries, and languages—the shifting opposite of my rooted friend. Walking with him through his parish, I am aware that the buildings and trees are as familiar to him as his own fingernails; that the people he throws a passing word to he has known, in all their changings, over a span of some fifty years; that he has surrounding him his own history and the history of the place, in memory and image, in language and stone; that his past is ever present to him, whereas my own is lost, shed. He has made his peace with place in a way that to me is, if not unimaginable, at least by now beyond me.

I spent a part of the summer of 1980 digging up Scotland and to some extent coming to terms with it, for although I have gone back to it at odd intervals since I first left it, I have always looked on it more as past than as present. My childhood is enclosed, encapsulated in it somewhere, but the threads that connect me to it have long been ravelled. When I return, however, I realize that the place exists spinally in my life, as a kind of yardstick against which I measure myself through time—a setting against which I can assess more clearly the changes that have taken place in me, and in it. When I go back, I am always trying on the country to see if it still fits, or fits better than it did. In one sense, the place is as comfortable to me as old clothes; in another, it is a suit that did not fit me easily from the beginning.

Still, the landscapes of childhood are irreplaceable, since they have been the backdrops for so many epiphanies, so many realizations. I am acutely aware, in Scotland, of how certain moods of the day will put me suddenly on a sharp edge of attention. They have occurred before, and I experience a time warp, past and present in one, with an intense physicality. That double vision is enough to draw anyone back anywhere, for it is what gives us, acutely, the experience of living *through* time, rather than simply living *in* time. People's faces change when they begin to say, "I once went back to . . ." Something is happening to them, some rich realization, the thrill of retrieval that pervades Nabokov's writing, past and present in one. Places provide these realizations more readily than people do: places have longer lives, for one thing, and they weather in less unpredictable ways. Places are the incarnations of a modus vivendi and the repositories of memory, and so always remain accessible to their own children; but they make very different demands on their inhabitants. In Scotland, the sense of place is strong; when I had left that attachment behind me, I had a loose curiosity about new places, and I still spark up at the notion of going somewhere I have never been to before.

Nevertheless (a favorite Scottish qualification), places embody a consensus of attitudes; and while I lived in a cheerful harmony with the places I grew up in, as places, I did not feel one with them. The natural world and the human world separated early for me. I felt them to be somehow in contradiction, and still do. The Scottish landscape—misty, muted, in constant flux and shift—intrudes its presence in the form of endlessly changing weather; the Scottish character, eroded by a bitter history and a stony morality, and perhaps in reaction to the changing turbulence of weather, subscribes to illusions of permanence, of durability, asking for a kind of submission, an obedience. I felt, from the beginning, exhilarated by the first, fettered by the second. Tramps used to stop at our house, men of the road, begging a cup of tea or an old shirt, and in my mind I was always ready to leave with them, because between Scotland and myself I saw trouble ahead.

When I go back to Scotland, I gravitate mostly to the East Neuk of Fife, that richly farmed promontory jutting into the North Sea to the northeast of Edinburgh, specifically to the town of St. Andrews, a well-worn place that has persisted in my memory from the time I first went there, a very young student at a very ancient university. I have come and gone at intervals over some thirty years, and St. Andrews has changed less in that time than any other place I can think of. It is a singular place, with an aura all its own. For a start, it has a setting unfailingly beautiful to behold in any weather—the curve of St. Andrews Bay sweeping in from the estuary of the River Eden across the washed expanse of the West Sands, backed by the windy green of the golf courses, to the town itself, spired, castled, and cathedraled, punctuated by irregular bells, cloistered and grave, with gray stone roofed in slate or red tile, kempt ruins and a tidy harbor, the town backed by green and gold fields with their stands of ancient trees. If it has the air of a museum, that is no wonder, for it sits placidly on top of a horrendous past. From the twelfth century on, it was in effect the ecclesiastical capital of Scotland, but the Reformation spelled its downfall: its vast cathedral was sacked, and by the seventeen hundreds the place had gone into a sad decline. Its history looms rather grimly, not just in the carefully tended ruins of castle and cathedral but in the well-walked streets; inset in the cobblestones at the entrance to St. Salvator's College quadrangle are the initials "P.H.," for Patrick Hamilton, who was burned as a martyr on that spot in 1528; students acquire the superstition of never treading on the initials. With such a weighty past so tangibly present, the townspeople assume the air and manner of custodians, making themselves as comfortable and inconspicuous as they can among the ruins, and turning up their noses at the transients—the students, the golfers, the summer visitors. Yet, as in all such situations, it is the transients who sustain the place, who flock into it, year in, year out, to the present-day shrines of the university and the golf courses.

The date of the founding of the University of St. Andrews is given, variously, as 1411 or 1412: the ambiguity arises from the fact that in fifteenth-century Scotland the year began on March 25, and the group of scholars who founded the institution received their charter in February of that dubious year. Such matters are the stuff of serious controversy in St. Andrews. As students, we felt admitted to a venerable presence, even if the curriculum appeared to have undergone only minimal alteration since 1411. A kind of wise mist enveloped the place, and it seemed that we could not help absorbing it, unwittingly. The professors lectured into space, in an academic trance; we took notes, or borrowed them; the year's work culminated in a series of written examinations on set texts, which a couple of weeks of intense immersion, combined with native cunning and a swift pen, could take care of. What that serious, gravid atmosphere did was to make the present shine, in contradistinction to the past. Tacitly and instinctively, we relished the place more than the dead did or could, and we felt something like an obligation to fly in the face of the doleful past. The green woods and the sea surrounded us, the library, and an ocean of time. When I left St. Andrews to go into the Navy in the Second World War, the place, over my shoulder, took on a never-never aura—not simply the never-neverness of college years but as contrast to the troubled state of the times. It appeared to me, in that regard, somewhat unreal.

In its human dimension, St. Andrews embodied the Scotland I chose to leave behind me. The spirit of Calvin, far from dead, stalked the countryside, ever present in a pinched wariness, a wringing of the hands. We were taught to expect the worst—miserable sinners, we could not expect more. A rueful doom ruffles the Scottish spirit. It takes various spoken forms. That summer, a man in Edinburgh said to me, "See you tomorrow, if we're spared," bringing me to a horrified standstill. "Could be worse" is a regular verbal accolade; and that impassioned cry from the Scottish spirit "It's no' right!" declares drastically that *nothing* is right, nothing will ever be right— a cry of doom. Once at an international rugby match between Scotland and England in which the Scots, expected to win comfortably, doggedly snatched defeat from the jaws of victory, a friend of mine noticed two fans unroll a carefully prepared, hand-stitched banner bearing the legend "WE WUZ ROBBED." The wariness is deep-rooted. I prize the encounter I once had with a local woman on the edge of St. Andrews, on a heady spring day. I exclaimed my pleasure in the day, at which she darkened and muttered, "We'll pay for it, we'll pay for it"—a poem in itself.

> It was a day peculiar to this piece of the planet,
> when larks rose on long thin strings of singing
> and the air shifted with the shimmer of actual angels.
> Greenness entered the body. The grasses
> shivered with presences, and sunlight
> stayed like a halo on hair and heather and hills.

Walking into town, I saw, in a radiant raincoat,
the woman from the fish-shop. "What a day it is!"
cried I, like a sunstruck madman.
And what did she have to say for it?
Her brow grew bleak, her ancestors raged in their graves
as she spoke with their ancient misery:
"We'll pay for it, we'll pay for it, we'll pay for it!"

And my father, who gleefully collected nuggets of utterance, often told of an old parishioner of his who, in the course of a meeting, rose to his feet and declared, "Oh, no, Mr. Reid. We've *tried* change, and we know it doesn't work." I noticed on a bus I caught in St. Andrews on my last visit, a sign that read "PLEASE LOWER YOUR HEAD"— a piece of practical advice that had, for me, immediate Calvinist overtones.

Some of that girn and grumble lingers on in the Scots. The choice is to succumb to it or to struggle energetically against it. Or, of course, to leave it behind—the woe and the drear weather—and begin again in kinder climates. What Calvin ingrained in the Scottish spirit was an enduring dualism. *The Strange Case of Dr. Jekyll and Mr. Hyde* is the quintessential Scottish novel. The mysterious elixir of transformation is simply whisky, which quite often turns soft-spoken Scots into ranting madmen. Mr. Hyde lurks in these silent depths. Virtue had to be achieved at the expense of the flesh and the physical world, in which we were always being judged and found wanting—the world, it seemed, had a vast, invisible scoreboard that gave no marks for virtue but buzzed mercilessly at miscreants. It buzzed for me. It buzzed for me and for Kathleen, one of my sisters, so regularly that we became renegades, outwitting the system when we could. In St. Andrews, that dreich outlook regularly took the form of an audible sniff of disapproval.

I was born in rural Scotland, in Galloway, in the warm southwest, a gentle, kindly beginning, for we were bound by the rhythms of the soil, always outdoors, helping at neighboring farms, haunting small harbors, looking after animals, or romping in the oat and barley fields that lay between our house and the sea. My father was a country minister, my mother a doctor. Summers, we shifted to the island of Arran: fish, mountains, and green fields. My father's parish had upward of seven hundred souls, in the village and on the surrounding farms, and, as often as not, my parents' stipends would come in the form of oats, potatoes, eggs, and game. When my father, from the pulpit, read of "a land flowing with milk and honey," I was overcome by the beauty of the image, and had no doubt at all that he was talking about where we lived, for one of my chores was to fetch from the rich-smelling creamery across the fields a pitcher of milk still warm from the evening milking; the honey my father drew, with our wary help, from the hive at the end of the garden. When we eventually left Galloway for the flintier east, a glass closed over that time, that landscape. We had left the garden behind, and how it glowed, over our shoulders, how it shines!

The peopled world, as I grew into it from then on, seemed to me to take the form of an intricate network of rules designed to curb any spontaneous outbreak of joy or pleasure. The black cloud of Calvin that still hung over the Scottish spirit warned us from the beginning that our very existence was somehow unfortunate, gratuitous; that to be conspicuous through anything other than self-effacing virtue amounted to anarchy. A God-fearing people—but the emphasis lay on the fearing. When I first took my son to Scotland, he asked me after only a few days, "Papa, why are the people always saying they are sorry? What are they sorry about?" About their very existences, for they are forever cleaning and tidying, as though to remove all trace of their presence, as though bent on attaining anonymity. Nothing short of submission was expected. It seemed to me that the human world ran on a kind of moral economics, entirely preoccupied with judging and keeping score, while in the natural world I saw harmonies everywhere, I saw flux and change, but I saw no sharp duality. The two worlds were out of key.

A college friend of mine who later practiced as a psychiatrist in Edinburgh was fond of saying that if Freud had known anything about Scotland he would have left Vienna like an arrow and taken on the whole population as a collective patient, to treat the national neurosis, the compulsive-obsessive rigidity that permeates its population. Yet as I look back on my childhood's cast of characters I am always amazed at what wild eccentricities the society accommodated, given its stern center—what aberrant madnesses it managed to domesticate. It did so by marking out certain wilder souls as "characters," thereby banishing them to glass bubbles of their own, and rendering them harmless. When I bring some of them to mind now—Pim the Poacher, who tracked down empty bottles all over the countryside and filled his cottage with them, all but one small room; Sober John, who read aloud from old newspapers in the market- place—I realize that the people of the town unwittingly kept these poor souls safe by wrapping them in kindness. (A sort of impartial kindness prevails in Scotland, keeping stronger emotions in check— the kindness that takes the form of an immediate cup of tea for the distressed.) But the turning of certain individuals into "characters" was also used to take care of dissident prophets and critics—any- body who threatened the unanimous surface of things. Similarly, at the University of St. Andrews, dissenting students, if heard at all, were listened to with a tolerant, kindly half smile. ("Thank you. And now shall we return to the text?") Such a society must inevitably gen- erate renegades, and Scotland has always done so, in droves—those renegades who turn up all over the world, not just as ship's engi- neers but in almost every outpost of civilization, where the cardinal Scottish virtue of self-sufficiency stands them in good stead.

There is also, I think, a geographical explanation for the steady exodus of the Scots over the years from their wizened little country. Scotland is an outpost—the end of the line. It is fastened to England, true, but not by any affection. The union—first of the Scottish and English crowns, in 1603, and then of Parliaments, in 1707—created an entity, Great Britain, that has never really taken, in any deep sense. To the native fury of the Scots, the English refer to everything as English rather than British, and the fact that London, the capital, lies to the south is a constant source of irritation. The Scots' resentment of the English is aggravated by the fact that the English appear not to resent them back but treat Scotland as a remote region, whereas it remains, culturally, a separate country. But the sense of being on the receiving end, of living in a country that does not have much of a hand in its own destiny, causes a lot of Scottish eyes to narrow and turn to the horizon, and sends a lot of Scots in unlikely directions, the homeland a far green, rainy blur in their memory.

I had no such coherent notions, however, when I made up my mind to leave, for I must have been no more than seven at the time. Nor was it a decision as much as a bright possibility I kept in my head. We had been visited by a remote uncle, Willie Darling, who had gone to live in Christmas Island as a consulting engineer, and who spent his week with us illuminating that place with endless stories, pulling creased photographs from his wallet, reciting the names of exotic fruits as we struggled through our salt porridge. What dawned on me then, piercingly, was that ways of living, ways of thinking were *human* constructs, that they could, and did, vary wildly, that the imperatives the Scots had accepted were by no means absolute imperatives (except for them), that the outside world must contain a vast anthology of ways of being, like alternative solutions to a fundamental problem. As that realization took root in me, I was already distancing myself from Scotland—at least, from its more forbidding aspects. I had no idea at all about where I wanted to go, or how, or anything like that—only that I would. And I did.

St. Andrews turned out to be my point of departure. I left it after a brief first year to go into the Navy, and by the time I got back, after the end of the Second World War, I had seen the Mediterranean, the Red Sea, the Indian Ocean, and enough ports of call, enough human variety, to make St. Andrews seem small and querulous. Yet the allure still hung over it, and I felt it still—felt the place to be, especially in the wake of the war years, something of an oasis. I have come and gone countless times since, returning, perhaps, because its citizens can be relied on to maintain it in as much the same order as is humanly possible. (In every town in Scotland, you will find houses occupied by near-invisible people whose sole function seems to be to maintain the house and garden in immaculate condition, as unobtrusively as they can. In New Galloway once, I watched a woman scrubbing the public sidewalk in front of her house with soap and water on two occasions during the day. She may have done it oftener, but I did not feel like extending my vigil.) The presence of the university and the golfing shrines has allowed St. Andrews to preserve a kind of feudal structure: the university, being residential, houses and feeds its students, administers and staffs itself, and so provides a pyramid of work for the town, as does golf, whose faithful pilgrims keep hotels, caddies, and sellers of repainted golf balls in business. Others retire there, to its Peter Pan-like permanence, bringing their savings with them. As a result, the place has a bookish, well-to-do air, a kind of leisured aloofness this side of smug. I liked to imagine the wide cobbled center of Market Street set with tables with red-checked tablecloths, between the Star Hotel and the Cross Keys, crisscrossed with singing waiters—Italians or, better, Brazil-

ians, carrying laden trays, sambaing, animating the place, rescuing it
from its prim residents, forever hurrying home close to the old stone
walls, eyes down, like nuns.

I do not think of the academy
in the whirl of days. It does not change. I do.
The place hangs in my past like an engraving.
I went back once to lay a wreath on it,
and met discarded selves I scarcely knew.

It has a lingering aura, leather bindings,
a smell of varnish and formaldehyde,
a certain dusty holiness in the cloisters.
We used to race our horses on the sand
away from it, manes flying, breathing hard.

Trailing to the library of an afternoon,
we saw the ivy crawling underneath
the labyrinthine bars on the window ledges.
I remember the thin librarian's look of hate
as we left book holes in her shelves, like missing teeth.

On evenings doomed by bells, we felt the sea
creep up, we heard the temperamental gulls
wheeling in clouds about the kneeworn chapel.
They keened on the knifing wind like student souls.
Yet we would dent the stones with our own footfalls.

Students still populate the place, bright starlings,
their notebooks filled with scribbled parrot-answers
to questions they unravel every evening
in lamplit pools of spreading argument.
They slash the air with theory, like fencers.

Where is the small, damp-browed professor now?
Students have pushed him out to sea in a boat
of lecture-notes. Look, he bursts into flame!
How glorious a going for one whose words
had never struck a spark on the whale-road.

And you will find retainers at their posts,
wearing their suits of age, brass buttons, flannel,
patrolling lawns they crop with careful scissors.
They still will be in silver-haired attendance
to draw lines through our entries in the annals.

It is illusion, the academy.
In truth, the ideal talking-place to die.
Only the landscape keeps a sense of growing.

The towers are floating on a shifting sea.
You did not tell the truth there, nor did I.

Think of the process—moments becoming poems
which stiffen into books in the library,
and later, lectures, books about the books,
footnotes and dates, a stone obituary.
Do you wonder that I shun the academy?

It anticipates my dying, turns to stone
too quickly for my taste. It is a language
nobody speaks, refined to ritual:
the precise writing on the blackboard wall,
the drone of requiem in the lecture hall.

I do not think much of the academy
in the drift of days. It does not change. I do.
This poem will occupy the library
but I will not. I have not done with doing.
I did not know the truth there, nor did you.

*

When the war and the University of St. Andrews were behind me, I did begin to live what looks in retrospect like a very itinerant existence. But there is a certain obfuscatory confusion in the vocabulary: people used to ask me why I traveled so much, and I used to say emphatically that I did not in fact travel any more than was essential—what I did was live in a number of different places, a number of different countries, a number of different languages. Writing is about the most portable profession there is, yet sometimes it seemed to me that I was bent on proving this to be so by turning my curiosity into a kind of imperative to go off and write about places that had whetted my interest. I grew used to being a foreigner, but I chose to see it as a positive condition, as opposed to that of the tourist and the exile, who are connected by an elastic thread to somewhere else, who talk of "going home"—a thing I never did. Disclaiming my roots, I elected instead not rootlessness, since that implies a lack, a degree of unanchored attention, but a deliberate, chosen strangeness. I felt the whole notion of roots to be something of a distorting metaphor, applicable only in certain rural contexts, like the village I began in. What I was replacing a sense of roots with, I felt, was a deliberate adaptability. I became enmeshed in the places I lived in. The absorbing present seemed to me all there was, and I acquired a kind of windshield wiper attached to my attention, clearing each day of its antecedents.

It was at this point, in the early fifties, that I stumbled on Spain— not by design, since I knew not a word of the language, or by any particular impulse the other side of sheer curiosity. From my first chance landing there, I was drawn in by a certain human rhythm, a temper that, the longer I lived there, I felt to be an antidote to my frowned-on beginnings, to the earlier wringing of hands. There is a frank humanity to Spaniards that makes them accepting of, perhaps even delighted by, their own paradoxical natures. Gravity gives way to gaiety, fatefulness is leavened by a vivid sense of the present. The people in the village we lived in in Spain had a way of standing on their own ground, unperturbed, unafraid, "listening to themselves living," as Gerald Brenan put it. They all seemed to me to be Don Quixote and Sancho Panza in one. They enjoyed occupying their own skins. They had achieved human imperviousness. V. S. Pritchett once wrote of "the Spanish gift for discovering every day how much less of everything, material, intellectual, and spiritual, one can live on"—a quality that appealed to me. And as I moved into the language more and more, I felt altered by it. To enter another language is to assume much more than a vocabulary and a manner; it is to assume a whole implied way of being. In English, if I get angry I tend to become tall, thin, tight-lipped; in Spanish, I spray anger around the room in word showers. Spanish, as a language, demands much more projection than English does. Hands and body become parts of speech. And then, of course, I began to read, discovering a whole abundance of literature that had been nothing more than a vague rumor in my mind. Spanish is quite an easy language to enter on the kitchen, or shopping, level. Beyond that, it grows as complex and subtle, in shading and tone, as any language does in its upper reaches. When I first met Spanish writers, I felt infinitely foolish at being able to utter no more than rudimentary observations, and I burrowed into the books they gave me, occasionally translating a poem, out of nothing more than zest. Translating was something that came to intrude more and more into my life, not so much out of intention as out of reading enthusiasm. But I felt in those first years in Spain that I was growing another self, separate and differently articulate. That experience was liberating, just as my first arrival in the United States had been—liberating in its openness and fluidity, as it is to all British people except those who cling excruciatingly to their meticulous, class-ridden origins.

I would go back to Scotland now and then, mostly in passing. It had receded in my attention, and I gave no thought to returning other than to reattach, in a fairly spectral sense, my irregular thread to the web of family. The point of going *back*, as I still said then, seemed an ever-diminishing one. People from my father's village, staunch citizens of St. Andrews, members of my family, even, would fix me with a wary eye and say, "You've been Away." I could feel the capital *A* of "Away" as a dismissal, a deliberate uninterest, and I conditioned myself to listen to the running account of local woes that followed. I would hardly have thought of referring to those occasions as joyous homecomings, although they had their revelations, mostly in the wet, soft, weather-stained landscape. They were nods in the direction of my origins, not much more. Scotland had become one of a number of countries with which I was comfortably familiar. I came across a poem by the Mexican poet José Emilio Pacheco, while I was translating a book of his, that so coincided with a poem I might myself have written that while I was translating it I felt I was writing the original. Here is my version:

> I do not love my country. Its abstract splendor
> is beyond my grasp.
> But (although it sounds bad) I would give my life
> for ten places in it, for certain people,
> seaports, pinewoods, castles,
> a run-down city, gray, grotesque,
> various figures from its history,
> mountains
> (and three or four rivers).

It was not long ago that my friend John Coleman pointed out to me the Spanish word *escueto*, deriving from the Latin *scotus*, a Scot. In present Spanish usage, it means "spare," "undecorated," "stark"; but when we eventually looked it up in Corominas' etymological dictionary we found that Corominas had an extensive commentary on it, remarking at one point: "[the word] seems to have been applied to men who travelled freely, impelled by the practice of going on pilgrimages, very common among the Scots"; and he gives the meanings of "free," "uncomplicated," "unencumbered," and "without luggage." The pilgrims obviously traveled light, probably with a small sack of oatmeal for sustenance. The word absorbed me, for it is clearly a *Spanish* notion, or translation, of the Scottish character— a view from outside, which chooses to interpret Scottish frugality as a freedom rather than a restraint. It was just the word for the transition I was then making. In Scotland, I had felt cumbered; in Spain, I was learning to be *escueto*, unencumbered.

*

In July of 1980, I returned to Scotland with a more specific purpose than I had had on innumerable previous visits: namely, to meet certain friends and dig up a small plastic box—a time capsule—we had buried there some nine years before.

*

By an accident of circumstance, I brought up my son, Jasper, by myself from roughly his fourth birthday on. Our existence together continued itinerant—houses, countries, schools strung on it like beads on a chain. We invented a way of life that could not have a design to it, for we had no points of reference. At certain times, pretexts for moving somewhere else arrived, and we grew to accept these as omens. Spanish was Jasper's first language. Born in Madrid on August 9, 1959, he missed by about seven babies being the two-millionth inhabitant of Madrid, whose population now exceeds three and a half million. We rented an old house in Palma de Mallorca from Anthony Kerrigan, the translator—a house in which Gertrude Stein had spent a winter, we all later discovered, a steep, cool old house with a persimmon tree, close to a *parvulario*, where Jasper first went to school, in a blue smock, as Spanish children all did then. Waiting for him at the end of the day, I would hear fluting Spanish voices telling alphabets and numbers, an awe of first school in their voices. We moved for a year to New York, where I would walk Jasper to school in Greenwich Village and gain a new sense of the city through his eyes. But my father had been seriously ill, and though he had recovered, I had the feeling of wanting to be within range of him, so we sailed to London, and eventually came to rest in a houseboat on the Thames, moored with a colony of other boats along Chelsea Reach. There we floated for the next three years. Jasper walked to a Chelsea school along the Embankment, and would report sightings from the murky Thames—once a dead pig, floating trotters up. We took the train to Scotland sometimes—that northward transition in which the towns gradually shed decoration and grow starker, stonier, the landscape less peopled. The boat felt to us like a good compromise—we could in theory cast off, though our boat, an eighty-foot Thames barge, would, once out of its mud bed, have gone wallowing down in midriver.

Flist, we called the boat—a Scottish word that means a flash of lightning, of wit, a spark. Many friends came to visit, some of them out of sheer watery curiosity. The boat rose and fell on the tide twice a day, and, with visitors, we would wait for the moment when it shivered afloat, for they would stop, look into their drinks, look around as though they had been nudged by something inexplicable. I was translating some of the work of Pablo Neruda at the time, and when he came to London he took our boat in with a crow of delight and ensconced himself there. He held his birthday party on the boat, a materializing of Chileans, and we had to fish from the river a Ukrainian poet, turned to mudman on our stern. Neruda surprised me on that occasion by insisting that the company return at noon the following day, without fail—not exactly a normal English social procedure. As they straggled in, he handed each one a diplomatic glass of Chilean wine, and the party began all over again. At one point, Neruda took me aside. "Alastair, you must understand, in your country people telephone, probably, to apologize for something they said or did; but we Chileans, we have learned to forgive ourselves everything, everything." I felt he was giving me cultural absolution.

The existence of the houseboat fleet was always being threatened by some authority: in the eyes of houseowners and solid citizens, there was something raffish, gypsylike, about our floating community, and we held occasional impassioned meetings, vociferously bent on repelling boarders. Yet on weekday mornings from certain hatches would emerge some of our number, bowler-hatted and umbrellaed, bound for the City. Jasper and I became enmeshed in the life of the river, however, and lived as though with our backs to London.

*

I often wondered about our shifting, our moving, and would sometimes bring it up with Jasper, obliquely, at odd moments. I worried about its effect on him, but the signs were that he traveled well. He felt no particular fear about changing places, and instead had become adept at taking on languages and mannerisms. Moving had sharpened his memory, and he would astonish me at times by his recall. He could evoke sounds, atmospheres, houses in precise detail. If I had told him we were going to Bangkok for a while, he would have immediately looked it up in the atlas, without alarm. I had to remember that in one sense he looked on places like London and Scotland and New York as foreign and strange, familiar though they were to me; but strangeness did not carry the aura of alarm to him— more the sense of another language, another way of being. I would concern myself with *his* feeling of rootlessness, only to realize that for him roots had little meaning. Not belonging to any one place, to any one context, he was in a sense afloat, and felt free to explore, to choose, to fit in or not—a freedom that in the long run made for a cool view. He did—and, I think, does—have a more intense sense of himself in Spain than in any other country. I had bought a small mountain retreat there in the early sixties, and although we did not go back to it with any calculable regularity, I saw how he lightened up whenever we did go. It was the only continuing past he had, and the villagers never failed to tell him how much he had grown, providing in general the trappings of childhood that our traveling life otherwise denied him. The house in Spain, however ghostly and remote it seemed to us from afar, served as the only fixed point in our existence. It was there that we took what we wanted to save—a kind of filing cabinet containing the keepsakes from other lives.

Our wandering life did impose certain restrictions: we could not, for example, have pets, because we moved in and out of the United Kingdom with such unpredictable regularity that the obligatory quarantine would have made them seem like children at boarding school. We had a more Hispanic attitude toward animals, looking on them as semidomestic creatures, whereas many of the English clearly prefer them to their fellows.

*

Inevitably—although there was nothing really inevitable about it— we moved. An invitation winged in to the houseboat one day from Antioch College, in Yellow Springs, Ohio (hard to find in the atlas), to teach for a year, and I accepted. We sold Flist, with many regrets and backward looks, and eventually shifted ourselves to a landscape new to both of us. The year was 1969, and the campus teemed and seethed; Kent State lay only two hundred miles away. Heralds came back from Woodstock with dirty, shining faces; no argument that year was less than elemental. At Antioch, we formed friendships that have lasted both vividly and ubiquitously; it was a year of fire, of passionate rethinking. Jasper trudged to a Yellow Springs school, and grew another American self, tempered by occasional nostalgic conversations and leavened by *The Whole Earth Catalog*, the handbook of the times. We had little idea of where we were going to go next, except to Scotland to visit my father, who was going to be eighty. So when the year ended we flew to Paris on a charter plane full of Antioch students chattering like missionaries, and wended our way north. To my relief, Jasper looked on Scotland as something of a comic opera, and I got glimpses of it through his eyes. He found its formality odd and stilted; he endured conversations that might have been scripted in stone. In a certain sense, he acknowledged it as my point of origin, but he made it clear that it was not his by suddenly speaking to me in Spanish in an overstuffed drawing room, out of pure mischief.

That summer of 1970, after spending some days with my father in the douce green Border hills, we took a spontaneous trip to St. Andrews. I cannot quite remember how or when the thought occurred to us, but then, all at once, on whim, we decided to spend the year there. I had some long, slow work to do, and St. Andrews boasted, besides its antiquated university, a venerable Georgian-fronted school called Madras College. On Market Street, I went into a solicitor's office peopled by gnomes and crones, and found that a house I had long known by sight was for rent—a house called Pilmour Cottage, not a cottage at all but an expansive country house, standing all by itself, about a mile from the center of town, in a conspicuous clump of elm, oak, and sycamore trees, screened by an umbrella of resident crows, and facing the sea, some five hundred yards across the golf courses. It looked across at the estuary of the River Eden, on the other side of which lay Leuchars Aerodrome, where I had first taken flying lessons, with the University Air Squadron, during the war, and which had later gone from being a Royal Air Force fighter station to the strategic importance of an advanced NATO interceptor base, manned by Phantoms and Lightnings, and consequently, I imagined, a prime nuclear target—an irony sharpened by those benign surroundings. I rented the house without a second's hesitation, and in no time we were lugging our worldly goods across a sand path that threaded through green golfing sward to take possession of Pilmour Cottage for the next year—about as vast an expanse of future as we allowed ourselves in those traveling years.

Of all the houses we rented, borrowed, occupied, Pilmour Cottage remains, in both Jasper's memory and mine, the warmest, the most ample. It had six bedrooms, a cavernous dining room with a long oak table fit for banquets, and a huge, encompassing kitchen, with a great stove like an altar, where we gathered to keep warm, and where we practiced the breadmaking skills we had acquired at Antioch. The kitchen window looked northeast to sea across the golf courses, and had a window seat where we spent a lot of time gazing. Day in, day out, in all weathers (and Scotland can assemble a greater variety of weathers in a single day than any other country I can think of), there trudged across our kitchen vision an unending plod of golfers, heads bent against the wind or frozen in the concentrated attitudes of the game. Jasper, bicycling back from school, would often turn up with a golf ball or two he had found on the path. We looked across at the square stone bulk of the Royal and Ancient Clubhouse, Camelot to all golfers, and we flew kites on the Old Course, their Mecca. It seemed somehow sacrilegious to live on the fringes of a turf whose sacred blades of grass were often clipped and mailed across the world as holy relics and not play golf ourselves; but we never got beyond acquiring a putter, which we would sometimes wield on the empty greens toward sunset, and an old wood, with which we would occasionally drive the lost balls we had accumulated into the whin bushes, to be found over again. The golfers were part of the landscape, like moving tree stumps; but one spring morning we looked out amazed to see the whole course dotted with tartan-bonneted Japanese, who had made their exhausting pilgrimage to play there for one day, and who insisted on photographing us as typical natives.

I looked from my workroom across the expanses of grass, sand, sea, and sky, quite often at the expense of my work, so mesmerizing was that landscape. Wind-bare, sand-edged, with clumps of whin and marram punctuating the expanses of rough fescue grass, the landscape had clearly brought the game of golf into being. The Old Course at St. Andrews has been both cradle and model; other golf courses can be seen as variations on its fundamental setting. The

St. Andrews golf courses, four of them in all, are grafted onto the town by way of clubhouses, golf shops, hotels, and wide-windowed bars—an enclosed world through which we passed on bicycles, still clinging to our immunity.

We settled into Pilmour Cottage as though we had lived there forever and would never move. All year long, a succession of friends came to stay, arriving sleepily off the morning train from London and opening their eyes wide when they saw where they were. We explored the countryside, we beachcombed, we sometimes even swam in the chilling North Sea. We wandered into the town and idled in bookstores, the stony town now brightened by the scarlet gowns of the students. Jasper took to saying "Aye!" and soon had the protective coloration of a working Fife accent. One afternoon, we opened the door to a young man named Jeffrey Lerner, an Antioch student whom we had not known in Yellow Springs but who was spending his junior year (improbably, to us) in St. Andrews, reading Scottish history. We all had many friends and turns of mind in common, and Jeff ended up renting a room from us, since we had rooms to spare, even with visitors. The arrangement worked wonderfully well from the start, for I was able to make some necessary trips, leaving Jasper in Jeff's care. Jasper was eleven at the time, Jeff twenty-one and the right cast for a hero, and I felt considerably relieved to have Jeff as an attendant spirit. I went to Spain at the end of the year, briefly, to settle up some matters in the village and to see how the house was weathering. I shivered in the stone house there, bare feet on the tile floor. Scotland was warmer by far, in a winter so balmy that we never once saw snow and throughout which we continued to fly the kites we kept building—elaborate kites, which stood in the hall like ghost figures and which we flew to enormous heights, sometimes even using them to tow our bicycles. Jasper and his school friends took over the outdoors and the trees, tracked through the dunes, and mimicked the crows till they rose in tattered black clouds.

Coincidentally, 1971 was the year Britain changed from its clumsy ancestral coinage to the decimal system. The *Scotsman*, our daily source of Scottish illumination, bristled with angry letters, and on the day of transition Market Street was dotted with dazed locals gazing at handfuls of glistening new change, holding up unfamiliar coins, shaking their heads, sure that the terrible innovation would not last. We hoarded the ponderous old pennies in a jar in the hall, and we had the feeling that the foundations were being shaken for once—that the past was, even in this everyday, metallic form, yielding to the present.

That year, August of 1970 until June of 1971, was the first I had spent in Scotland since I left it, and I found myself taking stock of it—as it, I imagined, was taking stock of me. The Hispanic world irredeemably alters one's notion of time, since it reacts instinctively, existentially, against the imposition of order from outside, particularly the order of the clock, and substitutes human time. Things take as long as they need to, and happen when they must. That had seeped into me sufficiently to make me intensely aware of the orderliness of St. Andrews. Something was always chiming. Punctually at five-thirty in the evening, the streets emptied; shop locks clicked shut almost simultaneously up and down the street. It felt like a place that had taken care to deprive itself of surprises. Jeff, newly translated from the Antioch of the sixties, could not believe the receptive obedience of his fellow students. As we settled into St. Andrews, the outside world grew hazy and remote. St. Andrews had domesticated it, making things predictable, untroubled. Yet I felt that, once again, sitting in the middle of the landscape translating Spanish texts, I was more estranged than ever from the formalities of the place. The presence of Jasper and Jeff, bringing back separate, hilarious stories from school and university, set me sometimes to trying to explain Scotland to them, and in so doing I came to see how little I identified with it at any point. It was the year that "Monty Python" made its first appearance on British television, and in their eyes St. Andrews felt like an endless rerun of the programs.

In April, the Argentine writer Jorge Luis Borges came to visit, on his way to receive an honorary degree from Oxford University. Borges was much affected by being in Scotland, although his blindness denied him the sight of it. He would take walks with Jasper or Jeff, talking intently, and recite Scottish ballads to us round the kitchen table. During the week that Borges spent with us, the official census-taker arrived at our household. The British are most scrupulous about the census, and the census-taker sat himself down at the long dining-room table, calling us in one by one to record not only our existences but a dossier of ancestral detail. Borges; Maria Kodama, his Japanese-Argentine travelling companion; Jasper; Jeff—I have forgotten who else, but I was the only mem-

23

ber of the household born in Scotland. As I showed the official out, he turned to me, scratching his head, and said, "I think, Mr. Reid, I'll just put you all down under 'Floating Population.'" He had a point.

My sister Kathleen lived in Cupar, some eight miles inland from us, and in the course of that year Jasper discovered relatives who until then had been only names to him. Kathleen had five children, who formed a rambunctious household—a family that in human energy far exceeded the sum of its parts, for it put out enough to light a small town. Jasper was astonished by his cousins. He gaped at the whole bewildering whirl of family connection. Our own family structure felt tame in comparison—ludicrously simple. The fact of his having been born in Spain made the others peer at him as though he might be an extraterrestrial. The astonishment was mutual, for my sister's children were voluble and full of questions. By now, however, Jasper had grown expert at being a Martian. His three nationalities—Spanish, British, and American—had made him a foreigner in every school class he sat in, and he wore his oddness quite jauntily. He was, I think, ahead of me.

An early spring brought greenness and soft air, carpets of daffodils surrounding the house, larks, hanging invisibly over the golf course, disappearing into song. The days lengthened, and the golfers played late into the long twilight. We discussed building a tetrahedral kite, modeled on one with which Alexander Graham Bell had once lifted a man, and Jasper looked alarmed. He played cricket for the first time in his life, with a certain disbelief. I came one morning upon a gray heron standing in the driveway like an omen, and we gazed at each other for a full ten minutes. Swallows and swifts appeared, strafing the house all day.

It was on one of those spring evenings that we decided, on the spur of the moment, to bury the time capsule. I cannot remember who raised the notion or why—it may easily have come from a book one of us had been reading, or simply from whim—but once we had the idea in our heads we scuttled about, gathering up elements of the place we felt to be worthy of encapsulation. We found an opaque plastic box with a tight-fitting lid in the kitchen cupboard, and we poured into it first the jarful of obsolete pennies and then the contents of a box in which we had kept all manner of foreign coins left over from various travels. We got together some photographs and letters, the local paper (the St. Andrews *Citizen*, which we read assiduously every week), other miscellaneous documents, representative talismans that we turned up at short notice. We realized that we had to prepare a note to accompany the scrambled contents, and it was at that stage that Jeff pointed out that burying the box would be fairly absurd unless we expressed an intention to dig it up somewhere along the line. So, casting about for an arbitrary date sufficiently far off in time, we came up with Jasper's twenty-first birthday, August 9, 1980—an occasion so unimaginably far away as to render us helpless with laughter, for then he came up to the height of the stove, and the thought of him tall and grave, with a deep voice, convulsed us all. We packed in the contents, signed our declaration of intent, made some notes on the day and on what we had just had for dinner, then sealed the lid on with epoxy glue. The twilight was deepening into owl-light when we went out bearing the box, a couple of spades, and a lantern lit for the occasion. It had begun to rain lightly as we crossed the front lawn and climbed over the wall into a clump of scrub and rough grass edging the golf course. We decided on that spot because it was public ground, and we wanted the place to be accessible when the time came. A small elm tree stood about twenty feet from the wall, so we chose it as our marker, measuring out an appropriate distance from it, which we all committed to memory, and set to digging. The box was duly buried and the soil restored—with unholy haste and an absence of ritual, because the rain was thickening and the lantern went out in a hiss. We hurried in to get dry, leaving the box behind us in the ground like a knot tied in the past to remind us of something.

Not long after that, a letter came inviting me to Mexico in the fall. It coincided with a vague plan I'd had of spending some time in Latin America, which Jasper had never seen, but with which I was becoming more and more involved, so, after Jasper and I talked about it, after he took a book on Mexico out of the school library and fixed Mexico for himself on his private map, I accepted. I had never raised the question of staying in Scotland, nor had he. Jeff was winding up his year, studying for final exams, making plans—first, to ship out on a French fishing boat, which he did from Lorient, in Brittany, and then to make his way back to Antioch, by way of our house in Spain. The end of spring was crowned by school sports day, the departure of students; my own work was almost finished. When Jeff left, the suspension in which we had lived all year was broken, and we found ourselves back in time. Our lease on Pilmour Cottage would soon be up, and I made plans to go to Spain on the way to Mexico, and once more assembled our worldly goods, dividing what to abandon from what to keep.

There were rituals of passage, leave-takings, last walks, backward looks. We had arrived in and gone from places so often, and seen so many people leave, that we were familiar with all the facets of departing. When the moment came, we took a long look over our shoulders at Pilmour Cottage from the Cupar Road, with a certain quick pang—the house across that low-lying landscape already half hidden in its own elms and pines, the crows hovering. Pilmour Cottage began to dwindle away in an odd kind of smoke. We had already forgotten the box in the ground.

*

For Jasper and me, the summer in Spain quickly became the present —a preoccupying present, because we were putting a new roof on the house there, sleeping, out of necessity, in the ilex forest, and catching up on village matters, changing languages again. Pilmour Cottage had gone into the archives. Certain appendages of it—a wooden spoon, a few golf balls, an etching of St. Andrews someone had given us in farewell—joined the array of keepsakes in the Spanish house. Jasper sometimes mentioned Pilmour, already handling the memory like a momento, a token. We caught a boat from Barcelona to Venezuela in early fall and made our way to Mexico. Jasper attended an international school in Cuernavaca, learning, it seemed to me, not much more than the Mexican national anthem, but that indelibly. We spent some time in Mexico City with the exiled Spanish writer Max Aub, an old mentor of mine—and an inspiring presence, because he was forever inventing imaginary writers, writing their works, and then entering into controversy with them. Late in the year, we took a freighter from Tampico to Buenos Aires, stopping, apparently at the captain's whim, along the South American coast. It was almost Christmas by the time we reached Buenos Aires—the beginning of summer there, which meant that all schools were closed. So during our time there and, later, in Chile—the hopeful Chile of Allende, before things began to fray away—Jasper went schoolless, but he was never at loose ends, for the Chile of those days made St. Andrews (or would have, if we had ever thought of it) more like an invention

26

of ours, a place we had once dreamed up, a place where nothing happened, as different from Chile as was imaginable.

After that long wander, we came to rest in London. It seemed to me imperative that, with such patchwork schooling, Jasper should finish up within one school system, with a semblance of order to it. So he went to school in Highgate and came to terms with England. Apart from irregular sallies to Spain, we stayed put for four years.

Jeff, meanwhile, had finished up at Antioch, had married Nora Newcombe, a redheaded and warm-witted Canadian girl, who had visited us at Pilmour, and who was doing a Ph.D. in psychology at Harvard. We did not see them for a long while, but we wrote when it seemed unforgivable not to. Then the work Jeff was doing— a Ph.D. thesis on the shifting attitudes toward bereavement in the course and aftermath of the First World War—brought them to London one summer, and we fell excitedly to filling in the missing time. With Nora and Jeff an ease of connection had existed from the very beginning, where we never tired of talking and noticing. The connection they had with Jasper was particularly important in my eyes, and I knew that it was in theirs: they paced his growing, their persistence as recurring friends a matter of great import to him, since he always had so many things to tell them, to ask them, when we met up. We had occasional, surreal, smokily distant conversations about Scotland; but we did not talk about the box.

I went to Scotland off and on from London. My parents grew frailer; my mother died, as emphatically as she had lived; and my father moved between the houses of two of my sisters, where I would go to visit him. On one of these visits, while he was living with Kathleen, I drove over to Pilmour Cottage, took a mooning walk around the house and climbed over the wall to the vicinity of the elm tree. The ground had a thick undergrowth, but I could still feel, at the appropriate distance from the tree as I calculated it, a recognizable hollow, a comfortable sag in the ground.

*

From 1970, five years passed without my coming to the United States—an unimaginable hiatus, for I had been in this country almost every year, or some part of it, since I first came at the end of the forties. I'm not sure now why that hiatus developed, except that we were more European-minded at the time, and that in London friends

27

from New York were always passing through, giving us the illusion of being in touch. I was working, also, through another long scrabble of translation, and I was caught up in the flurry of disaster that followed the coup in Chile—Chileans arriving in London, anxieties of not knowing—and in the obvious withering away of Franco in Spain. In the summer of 1975, however, some pretext arose for my going to the United States, and I decided to take Jasper, since he had not seen any of his American relatives in a long time, let alone the landmarks he remembered. New York felt sunny after London—not literally but humanly. I warmed myself with friends I had not seen in too long. Londoners are scrupulous about one another's privacy, and New York seemed loose and luxurious after the primness of the London years. We did, however, spend those London years in Victoria, a neighborhood that had become the headquarters of Spaniards who had left Spain in those lean times to find work elsewhere in Europe, so I shopped in Spanish at the street market, kept up with the Spanish football scores, and would translate the odd will or document into English for Doña Angelina, who ran a Spanish boardinghouse close to where we lived, and who knew our Spanish village well.

The United States this time had as visibly liberating an effect on Jasper as it had had on me at first gasp. I could see him taking forgotten selves out of the closet and shaking the dust from them. From this vantage point, London seemed suddenly such a polite place— if anything, overcivilized. When I returned to it, in mid-summer, it was with a surge of that extra energy I have always absorbed while visiting New York (though not necessarily while living in it). But I returned for a specific purpose: namely, to take my father back to the house he had lived in in the Borders, in order to give my sisters something of a break. Poor old man, he was already tired of his long existence, although he had bright moments. He rested at least half of each thick, green summer day, and again I found myself sitting, alone, in that shifting landscape, writing, wondering, while my father moved closer to dying, too tired, eventually, to say another word. He died as that summer mellowed into September, the way it does in Scotland.

> At summer's succulent end,
> the house is green-stained.
> I reach for my father's hand

and study his ancient nails.
Feeble-bodied, yet at intervals
a sweetness appears and prevails.

The heavy-scented night
seems to get at his throat.
It is as if the dark coughed.

In the other rooms of the house,
the furniture stands mumchance.
Age has graved his face.

Cradling his wagged-out chin,
I shave him, feeling bone
stretching the waxed skin.

By his bed, the newspaper lies furled.
He has grown too old
to unfold the world,

which has dwindled to the size of a sheet.
His room has a stillness to it.
I do not call it waiting, but I wait,

anxious in the dark, to see if
the butterfly of his breath
has fluttered clear of death.

There is so much might be said,
dear old man, before I find you dead;
but we have become too separate

now in human time
to unravel all the interim
as your memory goes numb.

But there is no need for you to tell—
no words, no wise counsel,
no talk of dying well.

We have become mostly hands
and voices in your understanding.
The whole household is pending.

I am not ready
to be without your frail and wasted body,
your miscellaneous mind-way,

the faltering vein of your life.
Each evening, I am loath
to leave you to your death.

Nor will I dwell on
the endless, cumulative question
I ask, being your son.

But on any one
of these nights soon,
for you, the dark will not crack with dawn,

and then I will begin
with you that hesitant conversation
going on and on and on.

Jasper finished school in London in 1977, and so we shuttered up the Victoria flat (which I had rented from Lesley, another sister of mine) and came to the United States again, I on my way to Costa Rica, Jasper to find himself a job for a year before going to college. I had been with him, mostly, for close to fourteen years, and there were moments at first when I would suddenly feel that it was time I got home, only to remember that there was no particular reason, no urgency. We were both relieved to separate, I think, for we needed our own lives, and Jasper seemed quite adept at running his. Time passed, comings and goings. Nora was appointed assistant professor of psychology at Penn State, and she and Jeff moved there, Jeff still lugging his thesis with him. I went to Brazil, to England. When I got back to New York, Jasper announced to me that he had been accepted at Yale. We could think of nothing to do immediately but laugh our heads off.

On New Year's Day of 1980, the day before I left for Puerto Rico, we had a party at my apartment in Greenwich Village, for Jeff and Nora were in New York, Jasper had a job in the city over Christmas, and other friends were stopping by from various places. Sometime during the day, Jasper, Nora, Jeff, and I found ourselves sitting round the table practicing writing "1980" on the white tabletop. It dawned on us all at the same moment, as though someone had tugged at the knot, that ahead, in summer, lay the box in the ground. We did our share of comic head-shaking and hand-wringing, in the Scottish manner, and then we drew ourselves up, Jasper taller now than we could ever have imagined, and took solemn vows to present ourselves in Scotland in August.

*

In mid-July, I prepared to leave New York, first for London, where I had to see friends, and then for Scotland, because I had not really been back since my father died. I had some work to do in Edinburgh, and I wanted to be sure of having a place to house the others if they turned up. There was a measure of doubt. I could not get hold of Nora and Jeff, who were somewhere in Philadelphia, and all I could do was leave them a message that I was going. Jasper was driving a taxicab in New York, and was rueful, in the way of students, about time and money. We considered for a moment postponing the disinterment until we were all more moneyed and more leisured, and horrified ourselves by the thought. So I left. I passed through London, took the train north once again, and landed in late July at Kathleen's house in Cupar, in the mainstream of a rained-out summer that was causing even the natives to grumble in disgust.

Kathleen and I have always shared an easy dimension. We forgave each other from an early age. She has a marked generosity of spirit, and is never still. To my astonishment, I found myself surrounded this time by great-nieces: my sister's two eldest daughters, Sheelagh and Gillian, had already had seven daughters between them, and there was a little army of knee-high girls whose names I had to learn. Sheelagh and Gillian had both married solicitors, both of whom worked in Cupar, for rival firms; Kathleen's husband, Charlie, was the bank manager. It all felt very dynastic to me, although at times it took on aspects of a Scottish soap opera.

In Scotland, the buying and selling of houses is generally managed through solicitors, and Sheelagh's husband, George McQuitty, handled such matters with considerable dash. In the course of doing so, he had acquired for himself and his family an imposing pile called Seggie House, built before 1900 for the factor of the paper mill at Guardbridge, four miles from St. Andrews along the Cupar Road. The sprawling house had a separate apartment, which I rented from George and Sheelagh. I had known the house under previous owners, but not as it now was, an anthill of activity. It had ample grounds and stands of trees, it had lawns, it had a huge, walled vegetable garden with a grape-bearing greenhouse, and it even had a tower, with a view of the Eden estuary and the surrounding countryside.

George, stocky, soft-spoken, has a quiet, burning energy, and at Seggie he was turning it to account. From a window, I would see him drive in at the end of a day, in a business suit and tie, and not five minutes later a chain saw or a mower would start up: George, in blue jeans, transformed into farmer. They kept pigs, chickens, geese, and three goats. George felled trees, turned hay, fed animals, rescued children. Everything we ate seemed to come from Seggie; what we left went back to the pigs. Sheelagh, in almost direct contrast to George, has such a vivid electricity to her that she seems to move and talk twice as fast as anyone else, and then she falls back into the repose of a smile. The girls descended in size from Jane, who, rusty-haired and serious, knew everything about "Dallas"; through Kate, moonier and more reticent; and Sara, four, with a piercingly unabashed curiosity; to Kirsty, five months old, who sat on the kitchen table and seemed to be fed by everybody. I never knew who was in the house—or, indeed, where anyone was—except at mealtimes, when they all magically materialized, as the food did. Sheelagh shot off somewhere to teach a class, to take a class, to exchange a child. The growl of the mower signaled that George was back. For me, in that humming establishment, writing felt like an indolent pastime.

I dawdled in Edinburgh—still alluring to me, a walking city. It did look dour, though, after New York. I went in to St. Andrews, called on some friends, bumped into others. They all asked me what I was doing in Scotland. I told the story once, but not again, inventing some other pretext. It suddenly seemed a rather weird story. August arrived. July, according to some accounts, had been the wettest in three hundred years. I had to tell the story of the box to the children, who thought it terrific, except that they doubted Jasper's existence, for they had never seen him to remember.

There is such a deep green to Scotland in midsummer; even in the drizzle, the greenness emerges, and much came back to me as I breathed that summer in. The countryside swelled with growing, and I sometimes drove through the small, neat villages of Fife: Balmullo, Ceres, Crail, Windygates—names my tongue knew well. Talking to George and Sheelagh, I found them cheerfully liberated from the glooms that still hung in my memory, although they were well aware of them. They also appeared relatively unperturbed about matters of money—a change from the frayed days I remembered, when it would have been unthinkable to buy anything without having the actual coin in hand, and when I once asked my father to show me a pound note and he had to go look for one, since he never carried

money with him. But then Scotland had badly needed not a genera-
tion gap but a generation gulf, and Sheelagh and George certainly
had as acute a sense of the world as anybody, brushing aside in-
sularities by ignoring them. They lived a thoughtful rural life—one
that was always being translated into activity. On some days, Seggie
House seemed as strenuous to me as New York.

I spent Thursday, August 7, in Edinburgh, recording a broadcast
for the BBC. I took a train back to Leuchars Junction, the near-
est station to Seggie House, and when I got to the house Sheelagh
met me in the hall. "Your friends are in the kitchen," she said over
her shoulder on her way to feed the chickens. I went through, and
there were Jeff and Nora, with children all over them. They had
rented a small car and driven up from London. By judicious phone
calls, they had traced me to Seggie, but their call had been answered
by Mrs. Trail, who helped Sheelagh keep the household back from
chaos, and her directions had proved unintelligible. They had had
to intuit their way. That same evening, a cable came from Jasper
saying he was taking the night plane to London and would call the
next morning. We sat in the kitchen and talked, the girls wandering
down from sleep on some wild pretext ("I just wanted to ask Alastair
something, honestly!"), not wanting to miss anything. Sheelagh filed
Jeff and Nora away in some part of the house I don't think I had
even seen. There was a thunderstorm that night, and in my sleep I
heard the goats bleat.

Jasper called the next morning around breakfast time. He was in
London with a friend of his from Yale. They were taking the train
up, and, with a change in Edinburgh, would reach Leuchars Junction
about eight that evening. Jeff and Nora, both goggle-eyed at being
back in Fife, went off to explore St. Andrews, suspending their dis-
belief. The girls were already enthusiastic about an obvious chance
to stay up late. But we kept studiously clear of Pilmour Cottage, as
I had done since I arrived. It was for the next day. We drove down
at sunset to Leuchars Junction to meet the train, which ground in,
salutarily late, and let out Jasper and his friend Allen Damon. We got
them into the Mini Jeff and Nora had rented, with some difficulty,
for Allen turned out to be six feet five, and intricate human folding
was required. We all ended up in the kitchen, eleven of us now, like
an assembled freak show, for the sight of Sara standing beside Allen
was comical. Jasper had a beard and looked tired. It occurs to me

33

that I have not described Jasper—perhaps because there are for me
so many of him, each separate self associated with a particular place,
each distinct in my memory. By now, he is about the same height I
am, just over six feet; physically, we do not look at all alike, except
possibly around the eyes, but we have a wavelength and a language
in common, which we fall into very easily. Sheelagh produced food
as she always did—less, apparently, by cooking than by willing it
into being. We sorted each other out, telling our separate stories,
everyone surprised for a time at the presence of everyone else, every-
one talking, a stew of accents. At some point, we made an agenda
for the following day: we would wake early, dig up the box, bring it
back to Seggie, and then make lunch, to which we had invited all the
stray members of the voluminous family that seemed to be sprouting
with the summer. George had already laid out a selection of spades,
shovels, hoes, and picks, and the weather forecast promised a fair
day, as they say in Fife.

*

Next morning, we began to materialize in the kitchen about seven—
Jasper and Allen last, jet-lagged. Over breakfast, we ordered the day.
The five of us would go, taking Jane along with us. George might
drop in later if we were not back. We folded ourselves into the Mini
and set out for Pilmour Cottage.

There was a new way into Pilmour, past a practice green; a park-
ing area had taken shape where our old imposing gateway had been.
But as we shouldered our spades, trudged round the perimeter of
bushes, and caught sight of the house, it all swam back, in a trance
of time. The house was white and well kept, the grass juicy around it,
the trees enveloping, the day, I am glad to say, dry, with a suggestion
of sun. Golfers were already out; it was a Saturday morning. I had
looked in on Mr. Stewart, the present owner of Pilmour Cottage,
at his store in St. Andrews, to tell him sketchily what we would be
doing, and he had been quite jovial about our return, promising us
extra spades if we needed them. We stood by the wall for a while
looking at the house, shifting it back and forth in our heads—all
except Allen, who had never seen it before. A sometime golfer in
Hawaii, where he came from, he gazed across the Old Course with
a player's awe. The morning was warming, and we were in no hurry,
except for young Jane, who could not wait to be astonished. So we

turned away from the house and found the elm tree, now grown into an adult elm.

It was at this point that a hesitation set in. Jasper, given the privilege, paced off a certain distance from the tree perpendicular to the wall, dug in his heel, and reached for a spade. "No!" Jeff was waving his arms wildly. "You've forgotten. It was three arm spans from the tree." And he started measuring off the spans. But whose arm spans, I asked him. Jasper's? He had been a lot smaller then. Besides, I told them both, I had been back to the site once, and what we had to feel for with our feet was a depression, a sag—as I began to do, in the thick tangle of undergrowth. We agreed, however, to start digging at Jasper's spot and then, if we did not find the box at once, to dig in the places that Jeff and I had picked out as more likely. Well, we did not find the box at once. We dug in a desultory way for about an hour, expecting with every spade thrust to feel a clunk of a kind, a plastic clunk. We found a teacup, unbroken, and a bent spoon. We talked about memory, leaning on our spades. Jeff and Jasper began to recreate the burying of the box, and even on that they began to diverge. Jasper didn't think that it had been raining that night, and hence surmised that the box must be buried deeper, about four feet down. I was sure of the rain, for I remembered the lantern going out. When we could not remember, we grew adamant. Nora and Allen went off to find some coffee, perhaps in the hope that, left to concentrate, we might clarify our collective memory. We did not. Jane pointed out where *she* would have buried a box, and she might well have been right, because although the presence of the house began to remind all three of us of innumerable details of the past, it did not tell us where to dig. A trance set in again for a moment. We dug more. I had broken ground where I thought the box was, although I admitted to feeling promising sags all over the place. My spade clanged against something—a buried can. Nora and Allen came back, and Nora told us about "state-dependent memory," which she elaborated on at some length. It beat digging. Although the presence of Pilmour Cottage was activating our general recall, she explained, we would have to recover the precise mood and emotion surrounding the event to narrow down our memory. But these were nine years behind us now. (She recently sent me an article from the February issue of *American Psychologist* that told me a great deal about state-dependent memory. It is something I have experienced a lot, changing countries.

35

When I go back to somewhere I have previously lived, I put my arms into the sleeves of the place at once, and find that I take on not just its timetable and its eating habits; I also experience moods heavy with dormant memory.) We laid out what we dug up, however, as methodically as archeologists, and we soon had a fair array of objects—more spoons, broken crockery, medicine bottles gummy with mysterious resins, a child's tin toy from nurseries ago.

Then George turned up, having already been to his office and subsequently sawed up a felled tree. (Jeff had earlier suggested altering a road sign near Seggie from "MEN WORKING" to "GEORGE WORKING.") George sized up the scene: we had already dug deepish holes at three points of a triangle of which each side was some eighteen feet long— so widely can memory wander. He asked us a few brief questions, then proceeded to excavate a trench, clearing off the undergrowth with a few cuts of his spade, and digging cleanly down, the walls of his trench exquisitely perpendicular and sharp compared with our molelike burrowings. He made us all tired, but we dug, scraping our way, as it were, toward one another. We leaned on our spades whenever it was decently possible, and looked at one another. It was time to be at Seggie for lunch. Spades shouldered, we stumbled back to the car. My instep hurt.

The children, far from crestfallen, were glad to have their anticipation extenuated. Kathleen arrived, with Charlie, bluff, looking not older but more so, as Jasper said, and Gillian, Fiona, another niece, Roy, her husband—here the canvas gets a bit crowded. But we ate well—salmon that Charlie had caught and smoked, a ham we had dealt for with a neighboring farmer, green abundance from the garden, raspberries that Kathleen had picked that morning. I sat on the step with Jeff a few moments. "Has it occurred to you that this could have a lot of different endings?" he asked me. It had. The girls had put out on the front lawn a table with a white cloth, to receive the box. We looked at each other, gathered our spades, and got ready to clamber back into the car.

It was at this point that George had a brain wave. A doctor friend of his occasionally repaired electronic equipment, and had, he remembered, tinkered with a metal detector for a fellow who lived on the far side of Cupar. He was on the phone in a flash, and in no time we were speeding to pick up the machine—which had been acquired by its owner, George told me in the car, after his wife threw her wedding ring into a field during an argument. They had not, however, found the ring—an ill omen, I felt. Nor did the machine itself look capable of pinpointing our lost box. We stopped at Seggie to pick up children, for Kate and Sara would not be left out, and neither would anyone else, for that matter, except Charlie, who was already sensibly asleep under a newspaper. We arrived at the site this time like an army, aghast at the chaos we had already created in vain. Jeff and Nora had somehow disappeared, strayed. But we began to dig again while Jane combed the promised ground with the metal detector. After a few excited sorties, we abandoned it, having found that it could not detect even a pile of change we planted no more than six inches down.

George, fortified by lunch, dug off in a new direction. The children pestered us with questions, and we began to feel a little foolish, particularly when a man who was visiting Pilmour Cottage wandered over to the wall. He could not contain his curiosity any longer, he told me, and when I explained what we were doing he looked at me somewhat sorrowfully and wished me luck. The sun was out, the day had turned glorious, Jasper had turned twenty-one, and we had dug up a patch of ground about the size, it seemed to me, of a small midtown office. And where were Jeff and Nora? George, leaning on his spade, looked a bit worn. It was the thought of unproductive labor that was bothering him, I think. It was bothering me. The children had extended our collection of relics considerably, by bringing in odd golf balls and empty bottles from the undergrowth. I hoped they were not losing faith. The clink of golf clubs and the thud of golf balls punctuated the whole day steadily, as golfers, unperturbed by our gypsy encampment, cheerfully hacked their way home. As Kathleen was preparing to remove some children, at a sign of lengthening shadows, Nora and Jeff burst out of the undergrowth, carrying what looked to me like a ray gun with a set of stereo headphones attached. It was a metal detector that looked as if it might have a chance. Jeff wasted no time in beginning to comb the ground with it. Even George cheered up. Nora explained. They had driven into St. Andrews and gone to hardware stores in the hope of renting a metal detector. An ironmonger in Market Street did not have one for rent or for sale—fortunately, for it would have cost about as much as a used car—but he remembered selling one last Christmas to a woman who lived on the far edge of town and whose daughter worked in Hendersons, the booksellers. They had tracked down the girl, got from her her mother's address, driven there, explained (I know not in what form) to the *dueña* of the metal detector—Mrs. Brian, of School-braids Road—and come away with it and more good wishes. At that point, Jeff whooped and jumped up and down, jabbing his finger at the ground. We dug deeper, for Jeff was still gesticulating. Another old can, but this one quite far down, giving us at least a glimmer of faith in the machine. As if to vary our luck, we all took turns, we all jumped up and down, we found seven more rusted cans. Kathleen sagely decided to go back with the baby, but the other children were still glowing, so they stayed. George's face had lengthened like the shadows. Around that time, Jeff and I began passing the metal detector (Adastra, it was called) back and forth between the end of the trench George had dug when he first appeared and the elm tree—closer to the tree. No question, there was an unmistakable hum, a steady hum, a hum that seemed to cover the area of the box as we imagined it. We whistled over Jasper with his spade. He dug, again; again, a bump—and we were on the box. We all stopped, Jasper scraped away the last dirt with his hands, and there it was, less than two feet down, not much more than two feet from the tree. It was slightly split, clearly from the blow of a spade—probably George's first spade cast, we speculated later. We lifted it out carefully and laid it to one side. It was six-fifteen, a golden evening; even the golfers, however, were thinking of going in.

Hilariously, we pitched in to restore a semblance of order to the ground we had combed—with our fingers, it felt. We had to persuade Sara to save only the best of our recovered artifacts. The rest we reburied, leaving the ground as level as we could, to go back to undergrowth. We wound our way to the cars like Millet peasants—tools shouldered, children carried—bound for Seggie. It was going on twilight by the time we got there. We decided to wash off before we got to the box, for none of us were regular diggers and we had managed to cover ourselves with native earth. My instep hurt almost enough for me to limp, but not quite.

When we had assembled ourselves, we moved the box into the dining room and clustered around the table. I had grown curious about the contents, because I had only a vague memory of them. We began to remove them, one at a time. First, however, on top, lay the card we had added at the last minute, before we sealed the box. We read the text aloud. It was full of ironies. "This chest," it said starkly, "containing treasure in coin and various souvenirs of the present moment in St. Andrews in May 1971, is buried here by Jasper Reid, Jeff Lerner, and Alastair Reid, in a spot known to these three persons." George smiled wanly. "It is their intention to return on the ninth day of August, 1980, to meet and disinter the chest in one another's company, and to celebrate their survival with appropriate ceremony. Sunday, May 30, 1971, a hazy day with sea mist, rooks, curry, and kites." And under that were the signatures, mine recognizably the same, Jeff's looking somewhat simplified, Jasper's in large, errant schoolboy handwriting.

We looked at one another. There we all were. We had survived even the digging.

The contents of the box, I am sorry to say, amount to a rather frail memorial of a fleeting time, but we took them out, one by one, dusted them off, and scanned them. Sheelagh spread a blanket on the kitchen floor, and we poured out the coins, the children running their fingers like misers through the mound of huge pennies, at last convinced that we had put in the day to some point. There were three small plastic biplanes that Jasper had reluctantly sacrificed from his toy hoard at the time; there was a photograph of Jeff, Borges, and Jasper taken at the front door of Pilmour, Borges talking, Jeff bending to listen, a miniature Jasper mugging at the camera; there was a postcard of the Old Course with an arrow pointing out Pilmour Cottage, a piece of white quartz, a leather pouch of Jeff's that had not stood the test of time as well as the rest of the contents, a copy of the St. Andrews *Citizen* dated Saturday, May 22, 1971, which we later read aloud. It might have been the current issue: the same civic preoccupations, the same cluster of local detail. There was a pen, which still wrote; there was an envelope from the Chilean Embassy in Paris addressed to me at Pilmour Cottage in Neruda's familiar green handwriting, a history-examination paper of Jeff's, a copy of the St. Andrews *Newsflash*—a small newspaper that Jasper and two of his schoolmates put out, and that ran for, I think, three issues.

There were separate photographs, too, of the three of us, taken roughly at that time. As we passed them round, I grew keenly aware of how differently we must be thinking, Jasper, Jeff, and I, about the piece of time that had passed between our impulsive shoveling of nine years ago and our laborious digging up of that day. For Jasper, it had been transformation—from oven height, happy and puzzled, in the way of children, to full height, a vote, and an independent being. Jeff had gone through the long tunnel of a Ph.D., and had probably changed least, in that he had an early serenity and his curiosity continued as alive as ever. Friendships we formed in the sixties, around that Antioch year, have remained very firm and clear to me, perhaps because, in that vivid time, the talk we had seemed always drastic, it gave off the same exhilaration that the war years did to the British, it became a defining time, and Jeff and Nora kept that directness alive: they foraged for wild plants, they read aloud to each other over the dishes, they took in the world crisply and intelligently, they thought of us exactly as we thought of them—as eternal players in a game of our own devising, fastened together by the habit of making every meeting into a celebration of that very happening, that moment. And my nine years? I had written a number of things, gone through the swirling glooms of translating, but what I think was most important to me was that after vacillating for so many years across the Atlantic, a transatlantic creature, I had shifted and had anchored myself in the Western Hemisphere. New York City is a good place to be when one has not quite decided just where to live—although I think that I have chosen looking for such a place over finding it. Apart from that, I had, as usual, changed every day.

So much for the contents of the capsule—not exactly a thrilling anthology of an epoch. But the fact that these inconsequential elements had lain underground—"all that time," Kate gasped, for it was longer than her life—certainly excited the children. In fact, at different times we all knelt round the blanket in the kitchen and fingered the coins—"the real treasure," as Sara said. The old pennies, some of them bearing the rubbed-down head of Edward VII or Queen Victoria in profile, seemed to animate us all. We rose on our knees, crowing from time to time. Fiona swooned over a twelve-sided threepenny bit from predecimal days. Sara was searching out the biggest and brightest—dinars, half crowns, and a single Swiss five-franc piece (which she pounced on like a buccaneer). I mooned over pesetas and duros with the obdurate profile of feeble Granfather Franco, whose death we had waited for so long. I left them to their scrabbling and wandered back to the dining room. In truth, nothing looked any the worse for nine years in the earth except Jeff's pouch, which had yielded to green mold. But it was the card I picked up and fingered—the card on which we had signed our names to an impossibly distant intention, opening a long parenthesis in time that the exertions of the day had just closed.

The children were radiant with the occasion, as though for once life had lived up to their expectations. The rest of us were tired enough to fall asleep in the soup. We ate up the delicious remains of lunch, to save it from the pigs, to take in sustenance. We had all-kept out a few coins, for sentimental rather than monetary reasons (although I admit to pocketing a sound American quarter, which had not aged beyond the point of negotiability). George seemed to me particularly broody—lugubrious, egg-bound, like the hens. We took a walk outside, he and I, in a night on which enough stars were out to confirm that they still existed.

"What's up?" I asked him.

We paced in the dark, ignoring the goats, the pigs, the chickens, the geese, the hilarity from the kitchen.

"The truth is . . ." I braced myself, for George, when he talks, is nothing if not blunt, emphatic. "The truth is, I thought at the beginning that today was just one of your wild inventions, that kind of playing with realities you quite often do. But, I have to tell you, it has affected me a lot. I went off and sat on a log and had a long think. I even wept at one moment. I began to think about Sheelagh, about the girls, about Seggie. I tell you, my life flashed before me, probably even more than yours did."

I was surprised, but not. George had looked all day like the practical digger, but I had seen that something was going on in the recesses of his being.

"I've decided something," he said. "And I don't think I'll tell the others until tomorrow. But that box of yours moved me a lot. I looked at Rona, the dog, and thought, Well, she certainly won't be here ten years from now. Then I looked at Sheelagh, myself, the children, Seggie, you, everything—heavens, it all seemed so frail and vulnerable that I decided, Tomorrow we're going to bury a capsule of our own. Ten years from now, Janie will be eighteen, Sheelagh and I will be forty, we move at such a rate that we're bound to be somewhere else—I don't mean physically, I mean in how we see things. So I'm going to tell them all tomorrow at breakfast to get things ready for a capsule, and we'll bury it just before sunset. Ten years seems a good time. Sheelagh and I have a twentieth wedding anniversary then, and

I know we'll still be married, still misfiring but married, and I just don't want this sense of continuing time to end, I just want there to be another knot waiting in the string for all of us."

I felt warmly toward George at that moment, but even so, I had had my share of time capsules for one day. I suggested we put in things from our capsule. Apart from the card (and what remained of Jeff's leather pouch), everything in it might as well go on in time, as far as I was concerned.

We went in. The children had claimed Allen as a private possession, and he rose to their demands. Allen had surprised us all, arriving as the only stranger at the feast and yet entering in with exuberance and good humor. He patiently pointed out Hawaii to them in the atlas and taught them to pronounce it correctly; he was for them too good to be true, better than "Dallas" (a rerun of which Jane had missed, unperturbed). He became their hero, far more fascinating to them than any of the rest of us—their parents, especially. "Wee Allen," they called him, to their own squeaky delight. We all had our fair share of blisters and aches, and I went off to bed. Jasper came in at some point and sat on the end of my bed, and we talked, drowsily, about the amazement of the day, of arriving after such shifting, such wandering. It was a point of arrival we would remember, a good moment to go to sleep on.

We all turned up in the kitchen the next morning in a fairly desultory order—at least until George came in and told the children what he had in mind. Immediately, they were seized with a kind of capsule fever and went off in all directions to gather treasures worthy of the occasion, piling them in the dining room. Summer had come out for the day—a warm, hazy heat, an enveloping greenness. Jasper looked quite dazed, grinning and shaking his head. Sheelagh shot off somewhere in the car. We interviewed the children with a small tape recorder, asking them what they thought they would be doing ten years from now. Kate said she wanted a baby. Sara, tired of being small, said she wanted to be as tall as Allen. We all added our own adages. George, who had not been about all morning, turned up with a fat sealed envelope and a brooding expression. I cannot imagine what he had written—but then perhaps I can.

The details of the day are blurred; about six, we gathered in the dining room again, and, through a rather painful process of elimination (it had to be made clear to Sara that if she buried her favorite small blanket she would, of course, not have it around), we eventually filled three vast plastic boxes, wrote out the appropriate documents, signed them, sealed everything up. The experience of the previous day had left its mark: we wrapped the boxes in aluminum foil for the metal detectors of the future, and picked out a spot equidistant from three trees—a holly, a chestnut, and a sycamore. George dug a deep, immaculate hole, and we all trooped out, planted the gleaming boxes in the bottom, took stock for a moment, and then shoveled back the dirt, taking turns to tamp the surface level. As the sun was going down, we lit a bonfire over in the grove where the goats lived, and sat about on tree stumps drinking hot chocolate, gazing into the fire, while the goats nuzzled our knees and nibbled at our shoelaces. One by one, the children began to droop and were carried off to bed. Jane looked rapt. I asked her what she was thinking about. "Nothing very much," she said. "But I like best of all being here listening to what people say." The fire began to die, and the dark came down.

*

That's just about it. Such a small event, and yet the ripples from it ran across the pools of our attention, stopped us, affected us. The next day, Jeff, Nora, Allen, Jasper, and I, after returning the metal detector to a delighted Mrs. Brian, took off for a five-day drive through the places of my past—to the Border country, drizzling and dotted with sheep, past the gloomy depths of St. Mary's Loch, all the way to gentle Galloway, grass-green, smelling of warm damp, to that village of milk and honey, to the house I was born in—stopping to see friends on the way. We told the story of the box in the ground once, maybe twice, and then we stopped, because it was complete in our minds and it was actually quite complicated to tell, as I have discovered. I have found that the telling resembles picking at a loose thread in a piece of whole cloth—seemingly simple to disentangle but winding in eventually a great intricacy of warp and woof, threads that lead in unimagined directions. I did not realize that in digging up that fairly inconsequential box, that whim of ours, I would be digging up a great deal more. Significantly, while we were digging that day away it was the roots that gave us the most trouble. But we covered them over again, and they will clearly endure. I think, in fact, that I am done with the metaphor of roots. I prefer that of a web, a web of people and places, threads of curiosity, wires of impulse, a network of the people who have cropped up in our lives, and will always crop up—"the webbed scheme," as Borges calls it.

There are many threads I did not unravel, many things I skipped over, inevitably, because I had not intended at all to wind in the fabric of the past—a precarious dimension, I think, for even in going over essential pieces of it I realize how much we all edit what has happened to us, how much we all make acceptable, recountable versions of past events. Mulling them over, as I have had to do, I find that sometimes the version and the grainy reality become separated: not contradictory but separated.

I have not spoken of many things. I have not mentioned money, for example. Living by writing, I had an income over the years like a fever chart, but there was always work to do, there was always translating, which I did as a kind of warm-up to the day's work; there was always enough to keep us going. If we needed money, I worked hard; if not, I idled. I have not mentioned various women, who moved in and out of our lives, who were woven into our existence, shifting, affecting. I have not mentioned solitude, which was an inevitable accompaniment to those years. I used to meet the English writer J. G. Ballard from time to time in London. He had raised his children by himself after the death of his wife, and he once said to me, "Remember if you are a single father, it's lucky you're a writer, because you can stay home all the time, you have the time for it." He always cheered me up. Nor did I feel so very solitary. Jasper was the best of company. But there was an essential solitude, the *soledad* of García Márquez, or of Melissa in Lawrence Durrell's *Mountolive: "Monsieur, je suis devenue la solitude même."* And I saved, on the bulletin board we set up wherever we came to rest, a clipping from an interview that Truman Capote once gave: "Writers just tend to learn more than other people how to be alone. They learn to be dependent on themselves . . . it just has to be that; there's no way of getting around it." The self-sufficiency was certainly something I had saved from my Scottish past–that and the fact of still having next to no possessions. Although Jasper alleviated that essential solitude, I fear that some of it has settled on him, by unavoidable osmosis.

I say "we" too often when I am talking about Jasper, but I have no intention of implying any unanimity of mind. We functioned as a unit, but for me the whole business of raising children meant teaching them to fly, separately and independently, getting them ready for leaving. I have been much preoccupied by fatherhood, for I felt most close to my own quiet father, and Jasper I have known as well as I know anyone. One moment lives vividly in my remembering. We had traveled up to Scotland during our houseboat days, on a visit, and we descended from the London train in the wan light of early morning, on the platform at St. Boswells, where my father was waiting. The train chuffed off, and, standing in the rising steam, there were the three of us: Jasper, small and eager, my father, pleased and open-eyed, and I, standing between them, father and son at once. That moment dissipated with the steam, and Jasper and I have exchanged the state of being father and son for that of inhabiting our separate solitudes.

And Scotland? It no longer seems a contradiction to me, nor am I inclined to rant about Calvin the way I once did. I have, besides, a stake in its future. On August 7, 1990, I have to be there, Jeff and Nora will certainly be there, Jasper will turn up from who knows where, Allen has promised his presence, Sheelagh will arrive, breathless but in time, George will have the spades ready, and Jane, turned eighteen, Kate, in a totally different shape, little sparky Sara, and Kirsty, who by then will be older than Jane is now—they will be there. Scotland has re-formed itself, in my mind, into the particularities of last summer, a time capsule in itself.

I call Sheelagh on the phone, tell her I am finishing writing the story of the summer. I have in front of me the card we all signed—Jeff, Jasper, and I—and a leaf from the elm tree that sheltered the box, already dried and cracking. A few odds and ends of the story are still lying about, untold. I ask her about the children, the goats, the household. She fires all the news to me.

"When are you coming back?" she asks me suddenly.

"One of these days," I say to her. I might have added, "If we're spared." I do now, but in the nuclear, not the Calvinist sense.

*

The evening I finished writing all this down, at the remove of New York City, resisting the temptation to pick at still another thread, and ready to leave Scotland alone, at least until 1990, I stopped off on the way home for a drink with two old friends, Linda and Aaron Asher.

"What have you been up to?" Aaron asked me, in a misguided moment.

I told him, in the briefest, most encapsulted form.

"But didn't you see today's *Times?*" he said, going to fetch it and ripping out the relevant page.

Here is the story in its entirety, page B2, April 24 issue:

It may be the ultimate skyscraper both esthetically and because of its superb construction, but the Empire State Building has not completely withstood the ravages of time.

A time capsule placed in the building's cornerstone on Sept. 9, 1930, by Alfred E. Smith, then former Governor, was removed yesterday in preparation for the building's 50th anniversary celebration next week. The copper box that contained the time capsule was full of water, and most of the contents had been destroyed.

The seams of the box, which evidently had not been properly sealed, had split, according to a spokesman for the building. The pre-cast concrete slab under which the box had rested had not been cemented into place. As a result, all the papers, which included a copy of the *New York Times* of Sept. 9, 1930, pictures relating to the building and paper currency from $1 up to $100—had disintegrated.

In Scotland, enduring is a much graver matter.

*

AFTERWORD

When I finished telling the story of digging up Scotland, I felt as if some ancient, dark creature had risen from my shoulders and flapped its ungainly way over the horizon. When it was published, I heard from lost friends—a bonus from writing. But, although the piece was finished, the flow of time did not stop.

In October of 1982, Sheelagh and George McQuitty sold Seggie House, writing into the deed of sale their right to repossess it for one day, August 7, 1990.

On December 20, 1983, Rona, the McQuitty's dog, died.

On May 14, 1984, Sheelagh McQuitty died, after struggling valiantly against an indefatigable cancer.

On June 9, 1985, Charlie Drummond died, cheerful, in midsentence.

On August 7, 1990, the rest of us did gather for the occasion. The company of children had increased, both in number and in size; but the absences cast a shadow over the day. The capsules yielded themselves up, easily and without ceremony, but this time they surprised us less. The children, however, were still enthusiastic over the idea of capsules as milestones in their existence, and set about readying another; but I chose not to contribute to its contents or attend its burial. The idea of a capsule lying in wait for me underground had taken on for me a sinister tinge; and besides that, I felt I needed no further extraneous evidence of the ways in which time passes.

Other People's Houses

H A V I N G   B E E N, for many years, an itinerant, living in an alarming number of countries and places, I am no stranger to other people's houses. I am aware of a certain disreputable cast to this admission; I can almost feel my wizened little ancestors shaking their heads and wringing their hands, for in Scotland, people tend to go from the stark stone house where they first see the light to another such fortress, where they sink roots and prepare dutifully for death, their possessions encrusted around them like barnacles. Anyone who did not seem to be following the stone script was looked on as somewhat raffish, rather like the tinkers and traveling people who sometimes passed through the village where I grew up. I would watch them leave, on foot, over the horizon, pulling their worldly belongings behind them in a handcart; and one of my earliest fantasies was to run away with them, for I felt oppressed by permanence and rootedness, and my childhood eyes strayed always to the same horizon, which promised other ways of being, a life less stony and predictable.

My errant nature was confirmed by a long time I spent at sea during the Second World War, on a series of small, cramped ships, wandering all over the Indian Ocean. Then I learned that the greatest advantage was to have as little as possible, for anything extra usually got lost or stolen, and we frequently had to shoulder our worldly goods, from ship to ship. The habit stuck—today I have next to no possessions, and I have closed the door on more houses and apartments than I can remember, leaving behind what I did not immediately need. If I had a family crest, it should read *omnia mea mecum porto* (all that is mine I carry with me); but it would get left behind.

Innocent in themselves, houses can be given quite different auras, depending on the dispositions of their occupants—they can be seen as monuments to permanence, or as temporary shelters. In Scotland, you find abundant examples of the first on the fringes of small towns, standing in well-groomed gardens, their brasses gleaming, their blinds half-drawn like lowered eyelids, domestic museums served by near-invisible slaves. When I first came to the United States, I felt it to be immediately liberating, in its fludity, its readiness to change. Few people lived in the place they were born, moving held no terrors, and renting was the norm. Yet people inhabited their temporary shelters as though they might live there forever; and paradoxically, I felt at home. When I began to spend a part of each year in Spain, my other adopted country, I rented a series of sturdy peasant houses devoid of decoration, with whitewashed walls and tile floors, and no furnishings beyond the essentials of beds, tables, cross, and chairs. It was a time when a number of unanchored people came to rest in Spain—painters for the light, writers for the silence—setting up working outposts in the sun, whose constant presence does simplify existence. Within these anonymous white walls, one re-created one's own world—essential books and pictures, whatever other transforming elements lay to hand.

In Spain, I grew very aware of houses as presences—perhaps the residual aura of those who had lived lifetimes in them, perhaps a peculiarity of the space they enclosed. I recall visiting a house in Mallorca in the company of Robert Graves, and hearing him, after only a few minutes in the house, making peremptory excuses to leave. "Didn't you feel the bad luck in that house?" he said to me once we were out of earshot. With time, I came to feel what he meant, not in terms of good or bad luck, but of feeling welcome or unwelcome in the houses themselves, apart from the inhabitants.

Of all writers, Vladimir Nabokov read the interiors of other people's houses much as psychics read palms or tarot cards: with a wicked accuracy, he would decipher absent owners from the contents of rooms, from shelves, pictures, and paraphernalia. When he lectured at Cornell University, it was his practice, instead of having a house of his own, to rent the houses of others absent on sabbatical; and behind him already was a wandering life of exile in England, Germany, and France, in rented premises. Summers he spent in pursuit of butterflies, in motels across the United States; and when, with recognition, he came to rest, it was in a hotel apartment in Montreux, Switzerland. These various houses and interiors inhabit his books as vividly as living characters—he is always making precise connections between people and the places they choose to live in, between objects and their owners. His *Look at the Harlequins!* is a positive hymn to other people's houses.

I know just what he means. The act of inhabiting and humanizing a house, of changing it from impersonal space to private landscape, is an extremely complex one, a series of careful and cumulative choices; and, in living in other people's houses, one lives among their decisions, some inspired, others hardly thought through. I make for the bookshelves with a crow of expectation, for the books, however miscellaneous or specialized they may be, always yield up at least a handful I have never read, or even heard of, and travelling has deprived me of the possibility of keeping a library, beyond a shelf of essential or immediate reading. Kitchens are a less calculable adventure. Some of them are like shrines, where cooking has been raised to a level of high art, and invite culinary adventure; others, incomprehensibly, are as bare as hospital labs in plague-prone countries, their refrigerators bearing no more than a few viruses flourishing in jars, two or three bottles of what can only be assumed to be an antidote.

At one point in our lives, my son and I lived in London, on a houseboat we actually owned, though temporarily, moored at Cheyne Walk, in Chelsea. We had three special friends, families that lived in other parts of London; and we came to an arrangement with them to exchange houses from time to time, for appropriate weekends. We had a loose agreement—we left behind clean sheets and towels, a "reasonable amount" of food and drink, and, for the curious, some correspondence that could be read. We all relished these unlikely vacations, since we left one another elaborately written guidebooks, and we could take in another part of London—markets, greengrocers, pubs, restaurants. I often wonder why people never think of doing that oftener, except at the wrong times.

In our travels, my son and I occupied rented houses and apartments from Barcelona to Buenos Aires. He can remember every one of them in detail, down to its sounds—the creak and shudder of the houseboat as it rose off the Thames mud on the incoming tide, a house in Chile with a center patio cooled by the cooing of doves, a cottage in Scotland in a wood of its own, guarded by a cranky tribe of crows, and the small mountain house in Spain that was our headquarters. Moving was like putting on different lives, different clothes, and we changed easily, falling in with the ways of each country, eating late in Spain, wearing raincoats in Scotland, carrying little from one place to another except the few objects that had become talismans, observing the different domestic rites—of garden and kitchen, mail and garbage.

Since the fifties, I have lived off and on in many different parts of New York, but very intermittently, since I came and went from Spain and from Scotland, never settling decisively in any one of the three. This fall, I returned from a summer spent in Scotland with no apartment—I had given one up before I left, and was expecting another in the spring; but a friend of mine, a dancer, was to be away for a month, and offered me her place in the East Village. I moved in, and took stock.

The apartment itself immediately felt lucky to me, the kind of apartment you want to stay *in* in, with high windows looking out over St. Mark's churchyard, and light filtered in through leaves to a white, high-ceilinged room, with about a third of the books new to me, and a long Indian file of records. I fell in happily with the place, explored the neighborhood, and found its Meccas—a Ukrainian butcher shop, pawnshops fat with the appliances of yesteryear, small Indian restaurants that looked as though they might fold themselves up after dinner and silently steal away. I made half-hearted attempts to find a more lasting sublet—buying the *Village Voice* early on Wednesdays, marking up the *Times* real-estate section on Sunday and then losing it—but that place made me immune to urgency, although St. Mark's chimed the hours in my ear.

One evening, I was having dinner with a friend of mine, a camerawoman, who lives in a loft in SoHo. She moves fast and often, and always seems to be attached to the ends of five or six active wires, so when we have dinner, we have a lot of ground to cover. Over dessert, she suddenly sat up straight. "By the way, I have to shoot in Arizona most of October. Do you know anyone who would stay in my loft and look after my cats?" We made a deal there and then; and, in a flash, I could see the shape of fall changing. Looking out reflectively on the churchyard the following morning, I realized that I was ideally equipped to be an itinerant. I have an office at the *New Yorker* magazine, where I keep books and papers, get my mail, and do my writing, when the time is upon me. What furniture remained to me now graced my son's apartment, and I was portable, to the tune of two small bags. I was in touch with other itinerants, some of whom would likely be going somewhere; and I was myself leaving for South America after Christmas, until the spring. So I dropped the *Voice*, and went back to reading Michel Tournier's *Friday and Robinson: Life on Esperanza Island*, my latest bookshelf discovery.

I had never lived in SoHo, and my translation there in October opened it up to me. I had to have a small course of initiation, in the hand elevator, in the fistful of keys, in the cats, and then I saw my friend off in a welter of camera gear—a less portable profession, hers, compared to writing. But then, I have always given thanks that I did not play the harp. The cats. Alvin, the boss-cat was called, a massive, broad-shouldered animal who looked as if he might lift weights in secret. Sadie, his sidekick, was smaller and dumber, but she simpered and purred, which Alvin never did.

Every morning, I fed them first thing, grinding up liver, cleaning their dishes; and when I came back in the evening, they would collar me and drive me toward their empty bowls. The first Saturday, Alvin got through plastic, paper, and close to a pound of sole when I wasn't looking, about an hour after his ample breakfast. But cats are unpunishable by nature, and we came to terms, which meant that I fed them just enough to keep them from breaking into those nerve-rending cries of simulated starvation. Cats in SoHo have the best life going, I concluded, in a loft that must have seemed like an Olympic complex to them, with me to do the shopping. Sometimes I wished they would go out jogging. But I found I could take a brisk walk without leaving the loft, and there was cable television, which kept me up the first couple of nights. Out in the street I learned to stroll all over again, and I connected up SoHo with the rest of Manhattan. I even took to working there, learning how Alvin and Sadie spent their day.

By then, I had come to count on what John Osborne once called "the blessed alchemy of word of mouth," that most human of networks, and it put me in touch with a poet-friend, who was to be away giving readings for a spell in November. Could I stay and look after their plants? Unlike Alvin and Sadie, the plants fed slowly, in a slow seep; and I grew attached to one small fern that required drowning every day, and that rewarded me with new green. Their apartment was in the West Village, the part of New York I have lived in most.

The stores were familiar, the kitchen a pleasure to cook in, the books unsurpassable, almost all of them good to read or reread. You can count on poets. Eerily enough, I had stayed in the same apartment once before, on a quick visit from Spain in the sixties, when other friends occupied it. Now it was dressed altogether differently; but every so often, I caught a whiff of its old self and experienced a time-warp, with the kind of involuntary start that often becomes a poem in the end.

As my days there were beginning to be countable, another friend called me, a woman who writes often on Latin America. She was going to Honduras quite soon, and she had two questions: Did I know anyone in Tegucigalpa? Did I know anyone who wanted to rent her apartment for December, while she was gone? Yes to both questions; and, a couple of weeks later, I gave her two addresses in exchange for her keys.

There was, however, a spell in November, between cats, plants, and travels, and also between apartments, when I was saved from the streets by being able to find a room on the Upper East Side. I was finishing a piece on writing at the time, working a long day; but even so I never became a familiar of the Upper East Side, never have. It is hardly itinerants' territory. People don't stroll much there—they seem more purposive, and you have to know where the stores are. You don't stumble on them. It was getting difficult, too, with the subways—I had to think, really *think*, where I was living, Uptown or Downtown, not to go hurtling on the subway in a wrong though familiar direction.

My last resting place lay on the Upper West Side, also a new territory to me, since I have always thought of Forty-fifth Street as the Northern Frontier. It was, however, a revelation. There were oases of movie theaters, comforting even though I never went inside, plenty of odd stores to stumble on, and the neighborhood, to my delight, was Spanish-speaking, even rich in Dominicans, the pleasantest people in Christendom. Moreover, a number of people I had always thought of as out of range turned out to live around the corner. I had had a hasty airport call from my Honduras-bound landlady that morning. "Just pile the papers so you can walk around," she told me tersely. Indeed, her apartment looked as though the negotiations over the Panama Canal had just been hastily concluded in it.

I cleared a camping space first, and then I put the place in order.

I have a stern morality about occupying other people's houses: I feel they have to be left in better shape than I find them, and this may mean fixing faucets or supplying anything missing, from light bulbs to balloons. What her apartment needed was restoring to its original order, now only skeletally visible. Anyone who tries to keep up with Central America these days acquires a weekly layer of new information, and her layers went back a few months. When I had the papers rounded up and corralled, the books and records in their shelves and sleeves, the cups and glasses steeping, the place began to emerge and welcome me, and I found, under the sofa, an Anne Tyler novel I had not read. One thing did puzzle me: as I cleaned, I came everywhere on scatters of pennies, on the floor, on chairs, on desk and table, by the bed. I could not account for their ubiquity, but I gathered them in a jar, about enough to buy a good dinner. Christmas was coming to the Upper West Side, with great good cheer; but so was the cold weather, so I went one morning, and booked my air ticket.

Before I left the city, I retraced my wanderings of the fall, going home again and again. If you have lived in somebody's house, after all, you have acquired a lot in common with them, a lot to talk about, from the eccentricities of their pipes to the behavior of their furniture. The tree house by St. Mark's looked properly seasonal, with a fire burning. I find I can still occupy it in my head, with pleasure. I went by the West Village, sat talking for hours in the kitchen, and then walked down to SoHo, where I called on Alvin and Sadie, who looked keenly to see if I had brought fish before withdrawing to rest up. I dropped off a winter coat with my son, and made for the airport and the warm weather with my two bags, leaving behind not one city but several, I felt, shedding a cluster of distinct lives. I just had time to call my friend, newly back from Tegucigalpa. Her time had been good, yes, she had talked at length with my friends, the apartment was great, thanks for fixing the closet door, I had turned up things she thought she'd lost, she felt maybe she had caught a bug in Honduras. I asked her about the pennies. "Oh, yes, thanks for picking them up," she laughed. "It's just that I throw the *I Ching* a lot. Have a good trip."

Waiting for Columbus

F O R   S O M E   T I M E, I viewed the coming of 1992 with a cer-
tain dread. It could hardly have escaped anyone's attention then that
on October 12th five hundred years had passed since Christopher
Columbus first stepped ashore on what was for him a new world,
however ancient its inhabitants. From the vantage point of Europe,
he began to make a vast unknown into a known, and the date has
been nailed down in history as that of the discovery of America.
Not surprisingly, 1992 lay steadily in the sights of many quickening
interests, public and private, and countless plans were laid to turn
the year into a circus of near-global celebration. It is understandable
that governments should seize on such occasions for a bit of national
brio, the satisfaction of having come a long way. It puts some kind
of affirmative stamp on a doubtful present; and, besides that, it gives
a year a "theme," which can be echoed inexhaustibly in exploitable
form. The year 1992 was a prospective gold mine: the books, bumper
issues of magazines, television specials, documentaries, simulations,
and reenactments, and the coins, medallions, ship models, maps,
museum exhibits, and other icons. One Spanish sculptor, Antoni
Miralda, set in motion plans for a symbolic marriage between the
Statue of Liberty and the statue of Columbus that stands on a cast-
iron column overlooking the harbor of Barcelona. Outsized wedding
garments and jewelry were put on display in various capital cities,
and the symbolic ceremony was held on St. Valentine's Day in Las
Vegas. It occurred to me that if only Columbus had had the foresight
to acquire the fifteenth-century equivalent of an agent his descen-
dants would have raked in much more gold than even the Admiral
dreamed of amassing, abundant though these dreams were, during
his various sallies westward.

Of the thirty-odd countries that pledged themselves to official quincentenary fervor, Spain outdid all the others in extravagance, spending hundreds of millions of dollars on the event. Spain, after all, made the initial investment in the Admiral's enterprise, and clearly looked to 1992 as a way of reaping even more than it already had from that first outlay. That year, Spain was the setting for a World's Fair (in Seville) and for the Olympic Games (in Barcelona), and Madrid was named Europe's City of Culture for the year. All these events attracted intrusion of tourists—tourism being an industry that Spain has been turning to great advantage since the sixties. Spain was ripe for a year of self-congratulation: since the death of Francisco Franco, in 1975, it has made itself into a responsible and sophisticated modern democracy, an active and energetic member of the European Community, with a new and zippy life style and an aggressive self-confidence. Spain trumpeted the quincentenary: in 1988, the Spanish government established a foundation in Washington, D.C.— SPAIN'92—"to engage Americans in a thoughtful exploration of the impact of Christopher Columbus' voyages and to strengthen the cultural traditions which unite Americans and Spaniards," in the words of its brochure. Spain also had built meticulous replicas of the three ships that made the first voyage—the Santa Maria, of a design the Spanish called a *nao*, slower and statelier than the caravels Niña and Pinta. They were launched by members of the Spanish Royal Family in the fall of 1989, and set sail in a reenactment of the voyage. Later they showed themselves around the Caribbean before turning up to lead the tall ships into New York Harbor on the Fourth of July. They were not, however, the only replicas of that little fleet; several were built—enough to stage a round-the-world caravel race if they all remained afloat after their strenuous year of simulation. One replica of the Santa Maria was built in Barcelona by a Japanese publisher, who intended to sail it all the way from Barcelona to Kobe, Japan, thus fulfilling Columbus's original plan, which was to find the trade route from Spain to the lucrative East.

Ever since the quincentenary loomed, however, there arose a countercry, close to an outcry, over the global fiesta, and it mostly came, understandably, from the countries of Spanish America—the discoverees, as it were, which were of course given no choice about being discovered. What came to these countries with the conquest was nothing good—violent invasion, massacre, enslavement, exploitation—and a number of voices strongly suggested that 1992 be observed as a year of mourning in Spanish America and the Caribbean. Cuba was scathing in its denunciations of the celebrations. I was sent a copy of the "Declaration of Mexico," circulated by a group for the "Emancipation and Identity of Latin America." To give the declaration's gist, I quote its first and last articles:

Whereas October 12, 1492, which according to a Eurocentric version of history was the "discovery" and/or "encounter between two worlds," marked the beginning of one of the greatest acts of genocide, pillage, and plunder in human history, and whereas the intention to celebrate its 500th Anniversary constitutes an act of arrogance and disdain for the peoples of the Third World . . .
. . . we have resolved not to participate in any activity related to the official celebrations of the 500th Anniversary, since such participation would legitimize the historical system of injustice and dependence initiated on October 12, 1492, and the spurious character of its celebration.

Rumblings from Latin America notwithstanding, the country that dressed the quincentenary in the most official pomp and gravity was the Dominican Republic, which, with Haiti, occupies the island Columbus christened Hispaniola—the first whole territory subdued and settled by the fortune hunters from Spain. Santo Domingo, the present-day capital, was the first outpost, the first colonial city in the New World, and its cathedral contains at least some of the Admiral's remains. (Havana and Seville claim to have the other parts in their keeping.) For the country's President, Dr. Joaquin Balaguer, then eighty-four, the quincentenary had been an obsession from an early age, and his long life seemed to have been single-mindedly aimed at October 12, 1992. As far back as 1986, Balaguer instituted the Permanent Dominican Commission for the Fifth Centenary of the Discovery and Evangelization of America—the longest and most pompous banner flown in the name of the event. He appointed as head of the commission his close friend and ecclesiastical henchman the Archbishop of Santo Domingo, Nicolás López Rodríguez, who viewed the landing of Columbus as the most momentous event in Christendom since the Resurrection. Balaguer clearly expected the quincentenary to bring to his country an attention and a sense of importance until now earned only by a rich crop of exceptional baseball players. Columbus, in his "Journal of the First Voyage," speaks of the island as "the fairest ever looked on by human eyes"—

57

an endorsement that is still used liberally by the Dominican Tourist Office.

The country certainly seemed so to me when I first went there, over ten years ago. Outside its capital and two or three lesser cities, it is rural and agricultural, dotted sparsely with small villages, outposts of subsistence, so that its beautiful and immensely varying landscapes always dominate. Dominicans are among the most cheerful people in the world, and I found myself going back to explore further. I eventually settled on the Samaná Peninsula, in the extreme northeast of the country, a narrow arm of land, thirty-two miles in length, that protrudes from the bulk of the mainland like a lobster claw into the Atlantic and forms a very long and narrow bay on its south side— a natural harbor that at different times has attracted the acquisitive attention of foreign powers, the United States among them. A low mountain spine runs along the peninsula, falling away on the north to a long sand coast and on the south to strings of beaches and small enclosed inlets. The whole peninsula is covered with coconut palms, whose easygoing crop has been for many years its principal source of revenue. Samaná is quite literally the end of the line: if you follow its single road to the tip of the peninsula, you find yourself facing a white beach, a reef, and, beyond, the open Atlantic. It was on Samaná that Columbus made his last landfall on the first voyage of discovery, and from there he set sail for Spain with news of what he had found.

As a place, Samaná is one of those geographical oddities which seem to invite a correspondingly eccentric history: it feels itself only marginally connected to the rest of the country; on early maps, it is sometimes shown as an island. A broad expanse of marsh—the estuary of the River Yuna, which flows into Samaná Bay—joins it to the mainland. In the past, most likely, the marsh did provide a shallow waterway across the neck of the peninsula to the north coast, an escape route for privateers bottled up in the bay when piracy was at its height on the Spanish Main. In those days, Samaná afforded just the kind of retreat the buccaneers needed; and, indeed, it has given refuge to a great variety of runaways in its long past. It has the look and feel of an island, and it has an islandlike history—a series of intrusions and violations, all coming from the outside. It is one of the poorest provinces in the country, with the leanest statistics, but the land is bountiful, and its inhabitants follow a way of life that has allowed them to survive, however frugally, for an immemorial time.

In the sixteenth and seventeenth centuries, Samaná was often raided by English and Spanish ships in search of buccaneers and runaways. It was not until 1756 that a group of Spanish colonists was shipped from the Canary Islands to found the town of Santa Barbara de Samaná. In 1807, while the French were briefly in possession of the entire island, General Louis Ferrand, Napoleon's commander in Santo Domingo, published a detailed plan for a new port, with a miniature French city neatly squared beside it, to be built in Samaná and named Port Napoleon: Samaná was to become a rich coffee plantation, Port Napoleon "a cultural capital between East and West." General Ferrand died, and the French lost possession of the island before the work was begun, but the plans for Port Napoleon still exist. Between 1850 and 1874, the United States Congress was seriously studying a plan first to rent and then to annex the Samaná Peninsula, and establish a permanent naval station in Samaná Bay. The idea of acquiring Samaná for the United States was something of a fixation in the mind of William H. Seward, who was Secretary of State under Presidents Lincoln and Johnson, and who had previously engineered the purchase of Alaska from the Russians. On three or four occasions, agreement seemed close, but Congress voted against annexation, and when further offers to lease Samaná Bay were made General Ignacio María González, newly elected President in Santo Domingo, took a firm and popular decision that no part of his country should be yielded up to foreign ownership. The Germans and the English had also shown a commercial interest in Samaná. Even so, the place was hardly prosperous: the population of the peninsula when annexation was being considered was under three thousand.

Samaná had received an intrusion of settlers in 1824, when President Jean-Pierre Boyer of Haiti, who had just occupied Santo Domingo, decided to ship in immigrants from the southern United States to populate the remoter parts of his new colony. Some three hundred of them settled in Samaná, and you can still hear the singsong English of their descendants in the market, or shake the huge hand of a man named Samuel Johnson on the dock. Don León, who keeps our local store, tells me of his childhood in Samaná, some sixty years ago, when there was no road to town and he had to row to market—a two-hour haul—sometimes twice a day. But he remembers a

59

Samaná that was more prosperous than now, with a chocolate factory, an icehouse, a soap works, and a busy maritime trade. Samaná harbor is now mostly a landfall for small boats making an Atlantic crossing or cruising the Caribbean. In January, when the trade winds are blowing right, we see them straggle in, flying a variety of flags, sea-weary. Last winter, I found a plastic pouch of water on the beach with instructions in Norwegian. I do not know Norwegian, so I added its contents to the sea.

It was Samaná itself, and not Columbus, that drew me in. Turns in the road revealed sudden beauties, to gasp at. Everything moved at walking pace. A car looked somehow absurd there. The place felt as if it were adrift, unanchored to anything. I explored the villages and the coast, I asked questions, I listened a lot, and eventually I acquired a piece of land just inside the point where Samaná Bay opens to the Atlantic: land that rose in a broad bowl from a small enclosed beach to a ridge, and fell away to the road on the other side; land that faced south across the bay and was thickly overgrown—well staked with coconut palms, all nodding seaward. Don Justo, who sold me the land, told me that he had not seen it in years, although he lives only a few miles from it. He had sent a man four times a year to gather the coconuts, but he did not think much else could grow there. Now he comes often, amazed that I have coaxed it into fruit.

In the Dominican countryside, campesinos live mostly in clumps of houses, settlements rather than villages—*aldea* is the Spanish word—that are dotted here and there, usually close to a water source. My land fell away steeply on the west side to a small, flat clearing through which a freshwater stream flowed by way of a small lagoon into the sea. Five houses stood close to the stream, accommodating in all about twenty people—men, women, a tribe of children. After buying the land, I made arrangements to stay in a room in one of the houses, and I hired the men of the *aldea* to help me build a small house, and to clear the land for cultivation. During that time, I got to know my neighbors very well indeed. We were some nine miles beyond the last town—that is, beyond public market, post office, electricity, telephone, hospital, and hardware store—and everybody depended on the small country *colmados*, which sold the basics: rice, oil, sugar, salt, rum. What we lived in—our bounded world—was, I learned from them, our *vecindad*, or neighborhood, which meant roughly the piece of coast you could encompass with a sweep of the arm from the ridge. Within the *vecindad*, you knew the inhabitants, down to the babies, and if you did not actually know them you had heard about them, in story form, and you inevitably shared their crises and daily dramas.

When you settle in a place, what you absorb, and to some extent take on, from those who live there is their vantage point: the way they see the rest of the world, their preoccupations, the web of their attention. Most of my neighbors are *analfabetos*; they neither read nor write. They are, however, passionate, dedicated talkers, often eloquent. Their mode, their natural wavelength, is to put themselves in story form. Their lives have no written archives, their years no numbers or dates; for that reason, a quincentenary is meaningless to them. They have saved their personal history in the form of a set of stories, well polished with telling, stored, ready. I have heard some of them recount their lives, a rosary of stories, on different occasions, and noticed how they vary with the telling. Everything that happens eventually circulates in story form, embellished by its tellers. Don León listens avidly to the radio news in his store and passes on his edited versions of it to his customers, who disperse it further on the way home. Traveling so, from teller to teller, quite ordinary happenings often turn into wonders.

In 1950, George F. Kennan made an investigatory journey through a number of Latin American countries. On his return, he wrote a report that was not circulated at the time, but that he refers to in his memoirs. I quote one passage:

> The price of diplomatic popularity, and to some extent of diplomatic success, is constant connivance at the maintenance of a staggering and ubiquitous fiction: the fiction of extraordinary human achievement, personal and collective, subjective and objective, in a society where the realities are almost precisely the opposite, and where the reasons behind these realities are too grim to be steadily entertained. Latin American society lives, by and large, by a species of make-believe: not the systematized, purposeful make-believe of Russian communism, but a highly personalized, anarchical make-believe, in which each individual spins around him, like a cocoon, his own little world of pretense, and demands its recogition by others as the condition of his participation in the social process.

I can feel the exasperation behind that passage: the exasperation of a diplomat accustomed to clarity; the same exasperation that travelers in a Western hurry will stumble over in Latin America. Yet

Kennan is putting his finger on a linguistic mode that is familiar to anyone who has lived in the countries of Spanish America, that I come across every day in conversations with my neighbors, that is at the core of Borges's writings. To Borges, everything put into language is a fiction, and should not be confused with reality. The fictions we make are ways of ordering and dominating the disorders of reality, even though they in no way change it. The "truth" of a fiction is less important than its effectiveness; and, since reality is shifting and changing, our fictions must constantly be revised. For my neighbors, their stories are a form of continuous self-creation, and a way of taming and domesticating the world outside the *vecindad*, the great, fearful unknown.

This fictive cast of mind, while it animates the *chisme*—the daily gossip that serves as our newspaper—is something of an impediment to serious discourse. I sometimes notice in the discussion I listen to on Dominican radio that what takes place is less an exchange of views on a given question than a series of restatements of the question, each distinctly personal, each with a neat resolution. It is perhaps too extreme to say of Dominicans that they are devoid of objectivity, yet that is what I often feel. It is as though they had no overall grasp of their own situation, even though they have at the ready a rich variety of explanations and personal remedies. For them, once a problem has been put right in words, it can be forgotten. The reality is another matter altogether.

Listening to the Spanish spoken in the Dominican Republic, I quite often come on words so bizarrely unfamiliar that I have to reach their meaning by scrutinous questioning, for I have never heard them anywhere else. One such word, of Afro-Hispanic origin, from the language arrived at by the Africans brought as slaves to Hispaniola, is the noun *fucú* or *fukú*. It is often spoken with a certain dropping of the voice. *Un fucú* is something ill-omened, likely to bring bad luck, something in a person or a place or a happening that has doom about it. At the materialization of a *fucú* in any form, Dominicans cross their index fingers in the air and exclaim "*Zafa!*"—loosely translated as "Change the subject." At least they used to, I am told by the elders in my neighborhood: perhaps the custom has waned because there are so many obvious public *fucús* in the country now that the day would be one long "*Zafa!*" The word has entered not just my vocabulary but my consciousness; I am able to realize that some people and elements in New York have a *fucú* about them for me. It helps me save time.

The most interesting *fucú* of all among Dominicans, however, is the superstition that has existed for centuries that bad luck would dog anyone who spoke aloud the name of Cristóbal Colón. That called for instant crossed fingers and a loud "*Zafa!*" One referred instead to the Admiral, or the Discoverer. The official propaganda surrounding the quincentenary has had to face down the *fucú*, as it were, for the name has somehow kept coming up. But the campesinos still believe in the *fucú* that C——— C——— brings bad luck, perhaps with more fervor now than before. One of my neighbors told me solemnly that the word *colonia*—"colony"—came from the name of Cristóbal Colón, an error I saw no point in correcting.

In the evenings of those first days, when we had finished work and bathed and eaten, we would sit by the stream and talk as the dark came down. My neighbors were full of questions, mostly about life in the United States, which I answered with some care; and in my turn I questioned them closely about their lives and the ways of the place. We have continued so ever since. In the evenings I hear feet on the stones of my terrace, and someone will materialize, always with an offering—Sandro with fish, Felipe with an egg—and we will sit on the warm stone and talk. A kind of natural barter plays a large part in my neighbors' existence, and, indeed, they like nothing better than a "deal," an exchange that pleases both sides. I have to remember that I am a *patrón*, a landowner, and I have to assume the role sometimes: to settle a dispute, or to come up with money for medicine—a debt that is always paid off with a day's work. Dominican society is a curious web of family connections, of debts and favors owed, of patronage and reward—a system that, while it functions well enough in remote country settlements like ours, has turned Dominican politics into a tangle of corruption. My neighbors are natural anarchists. Pucho, who has worked with me since the beginning, and now lives, with his family, on the land above mine, insists that he has no loyalties other than to what his eye encompasses, and he leaves no ground unplanted, for that is what makes unquestionable sense to him. One evening, he found, in a catalogue that had come with my mail, a rowing machine. He was delighted, for he has a long row to the reef where he goes fishing, and hates rowing; when

I explained that people in cities had rowing machines in their houses to keep healthy, he looked at my pityingly.

As I discovered by the stream, history for my neighbors is mostly hearsay, vague rumblings in a dateless clutter of past, anchored by a few facts brought home from school by the children. For most of them, the past, though it has engendered their present, is an irrelevance. So at one point, for a few evenings running, I told them a fairly simplified version, though quite a detailed one, of Cristóbal Colón and the first voyage, the first landings, the coming of the Spaniards, and the subsequent enslavement of their country. I told them what I knew about the Indians—the Tainos and the Ciguayos—who when Colón arrived had been living an unvarying rural existence. They made their settlements by fresh water, close to the sea. They fished, they bartered work and harvests, they lived communally. They were also innocent of money, as my neighbors often are, though not from choice.

Some of my neighbors became quite indignant at my version of the arrival of the Spaniards, and, indeed, I did myself. Although I had read fairly extensively about the conquest, I had always done so in the historical mass, so to speak; I had never been physically close to the scene before, and I felt myself suddenly waking up to those happenings as quite easily imaginable realities. When the house was finished and the books were unpacked, I started to read that history all over again, beginning with where I was—with Columbus's landing on Samaná—and then going mostly backward, reading what I could find about the conditions of life in Hispaniola before that catastrophic disembarkation.

In early January of 1493, aboard the Niña, with the Pinta in attendance, Columbus was bowling along the north coast of Hispaniola, on an easterly course. Of all his landfalls so far, Hispaniola had proved the most rewarding. Its natives were friendly and docile, its vegetation was sumptuous, and he had found enough gold to fuel expectations of more. It would be his territory, he had decided, his base for any future exploration. Fixed firmly in his sailing mind, however, was the urge to return to Spain with all dispatch, on the first good wind. He had lost the Santa María, grounded on a coral reef on Christmas Eve, but its timbers had been used to build a small fort called La Navidad, where the Admiral left behind a garrison of thirty-nine men. The standard histories have him rounding the northeast corner of the Samaná Peninsula and deciding to make one last landfall, to take on fresh water and provisions for the return crossing, and, if possible, to careen and caulk his two remaining boats, which were taking water. According to his log entry for January 12, 1493, the two ships entered "an enormous bay three leagues wide, with a little island [*una isleta pequeñuela*], in the middle of it," and they anchored between the little island and a shallow sand beach. The following morning, the Admiral sent a boat ashore to treat with the Indians, as he had been doing with regularity over the past three months. These Indians, however, were quite different in appearance from the ones so far encountered. These wore their hair long, plaited with bird plumage, and they blackened their faces. Also, unlike most of those so far encountered, they carried arms— longbows and arrows. The crew persuaded one of them to return to the ship and talk with the Admiral. By this time, the Spaniards had most likely acquired a certain basic vocabulary, and, as usual, the Admiral questioned the man assiduously on the whereabouts of gold, and delivered an invitation to his cacique, his chief. The Indian was fed, given some trinkets, and returned by the boat's crew to his beach. On this occasion, some fifty-five Indians had gathered, and seven of the boat's crew bargained for bows and arrows, as they had been ordered. They had acquired two bows when something caused the Indians to go back to collect their arms. Leaving nothing to chance, the seven Spaniards attacked them, wounding one Indian with a sword slash in the buttocks and another in the breast with a crossbow arrow. This brief skirmish, most likely founded on a misunderstanding, has gone into the annals as the first shedding of indigenous blood in the New World—the first, faint inkling of the slaughter that was to follow. Three days later, the wind turned westerly, and, with four of the long-haired Indians added to the onboard evidence of the New World, the Niña and the Pinta put out well before dawn and set course for Spain. In his log the Admiral referred to his last anchorage as the Golfo de las Flechas, the Bay of the Arrows.

"The Journal of the First Voyage," the written source of the discovery, is a strangely diffuse document, very far from objectivity even when it is being a ship's log, for some of its landfalls are still being argued over. (There is no original of the document. The version we read is an annotated text of a 1530s edition prepared and in many instances paraphrased by a later visitor, the diligent friar Bartolomé de Las Casas, from a less than complete copy made by an errant scribe; but not even this text was known about until 1825, when it was published, circulated, studied, and, in 1828, translated into English.) Some of the journal is first person, some third person (Las Casas' paraphrase), some in the shorthand of terse nautical observation. Columbus's own observations sometimes have the true awe of a man seeing unimagined wonders for the first time, but they are interspersed with passages of self-congratulation, lavish reassurances to Their Majesties, small sermons and other bursts of missionary zeal, inflated promises of bountiful gold, and a very eccentric geography. Columbus was in his forties by then, and for the last ten years his sole preoccupation had been to persuade some rich and powerful patron to underwrite an expedition of discovery. He had presented his arguments many times—as often as possible—first to the Portuguese court and then to Their Catholic Majesties in Spain, and he had obviously made them as alluring as he could. He was familiar with Marco Polo's chronicles, and cast his own expectations in the same high tone, conjuring up a vision of a New World that, since it was so far entirely imagined, could be wondrous in every respect. He became a practiced exaggerator. He was shrewd enough to realize that he had to satisfy a multitude of interests, and his arguments were consequently many-facetted: for mercantile interests he would discover the route to the East that would open up trade with Cathay and with Cipango (Japan); for the Crown he would claim all new lands and found for Spain a colonial empire; for the Church he could promise converts, he would find the Garden of Eden; and beyond all these interests he dangled the promise of gold in abundance, at a time when Spain's treasury was exhausted. He had voiced these expectations so often that when he did find land what he looked for first was a self-justifying confirmation of them. His New World existed for him in the fiction he had made of it before he discovered it, and there was often a considerable disparity between what he found and what he said he found. After exploring the coast of Cuba, in November, he insisted, and continued to insist, that it was Cathay; yet he did not continue west. By then, from the natives he encountered he had picked up enough stories of gold so that it was fixed abidingly in the forefront of his attention. For him, the rumor of gold brought wish and reality together. Forgetting about the East, he followed the Indians' indications and turned back in the direction of Hispaniola.

Among a handful of anecdotes that Dominicans like to tell about the conquest is one that I have heard in a few variant forms. As fact it is improbable, but as essence it is peerless. It became the practice of the caciques to retreat from the arriving Spaniards, leaving placatory gifts in their path. The story has one such cacique leaving as an offering his beautiful daughter, bound to a stake, and wearing nothing but a gold ring in her nose. The Admiral, arriving at the head of his men, stops them suddenly with spread hands, gazes at the girl for a gravid minute, then points a trembling finger and asks, "Where did you get that ring?"

I keep thinking of those first encounters, particularly from the point of view of language. The Spaniards and the Indians had no language in common, and Columbus had to communicate as tourists do nowadays in markets beyond their linguistic reach—by pointing and gesticulating. While that probably served well enough to get the ships' companies food and water, to make gestures of friendship and good intentions, and even to emphasize a particularly urgent interest in anything made of gold, it cannot have made possible the communication of anything abstract, like the claiming of all the Indians' lands in the name of Ferdinand and Isabella, or the fundamental tenets of the Holy Roman Church. Over various landfalls, the Spaniards probably began to assemble a sketchy vocabulary of native words, but there are signs in the journal that Columbus was prone to the affliction of beginners in any language—an overwillingness to understand. Hearsay for Columbus was whatever he thought he heard, and hearsay was the basis of his golden promises in a famous letter that he addressed to Their Majesties on the return crossing. Besides the gold and the Indians, Columbus was carrying back with him a great fund of information that he had sifted from the Indians' stories, some of it more imagined than real. "The Journal of the First Voyage" has a kind of speculative edge to it, an awe in its voice, a looking-at that before very long became a looking-for. The second voyage, from 1493 to 1496, was no longer looking for gold; it was going after it. With the second voyage, the conquest really began.

On the first voyage, Columbus went through an orgy of naming—christening capes, headlands, bays, points, rivers, and islands, and entering the names meticulously in his log. For him, giving them

Spanish names was synonymous with claiming them for Spain, and his naming grew more diligent as the voyage progressed. No matter that everything was already named and understood by the Indians— from now on, Spain was to impose itself on Hispaniola, a God-appointed enterprise. Whatever form of life the Indians had achieved up until now was an irrelevance, since it was about to be ended, irrevocably.

The landfall in Columbus's Bay of the Arrows, of first-blood fame, is identified in the vast majority of books about Columbus as the beach called Las Flechas, on the south coast of the Samaná Peninsula. Facing that beach is a small, neat jewel of an island known as Cayo Levantado, assumed to be the "little island" Columbus identifies in his log. Las Flechas lies along the coast from our beach, about a mile farther into the bay, and I must have passed it hundreds of times by now, for the road to town runs just above it. It has served to keep Columbus on my mind. The first time I explored it, I looked for some kind of marker, since Columbus's landfalls have been well labeled, but it was as anonymous as when he found it. Beyond a broad, untidy straggle of coconut palms, which always cast for me a kind of cathedral gloom on the beaches below them, lay its curve of sand, three small fishing boats pulled up, a litter of fishing gear, and Cayo Levantado riding at anchor about a mile offshore. I talked to an old man who was resting his back against one of the boats. I asked him about the beach and Columbus. "Colón? Colón? Now, I've heard that name."

Since about the first century, Arawak Indians had been migrating north from the South American continent through the islands, and so had settled Hispaniola a good many centuries before Columbus arrived. Those island Arawaks of Hispaniola are now generally referred to as Tainos, from the name for their upper class, for, although they had originally brought with them their own plants and methods of cultivation, they evolved a way of life distinct to the island. What we know of their mode of existence in Hispaniola has reached us mainly through the assiduousness of four chroniclers who came on subsequent voyages—Bartolomé de Las Casas, Peter Martyr, Guillermo Coma, and Gonzalo Fernández de Oviedo. Yet the more I read in the chronicles about how the Tainos lived, the more I realize that their life resembled, in most of its fundamentals, the present life of our *vecindad*. Taino artifacts are everywhere—the neighbors will bring me pieces of red pottery they come across, or an axe head, still lime-encrusted. Their life-sustaining crop was the root cassava—manioc, yucca, tapioca. It gave them bread, and they grew it in conelike mounds of earth called *conucos*. Cassava, yams, and sweet potato, along with beans, maize, peppers, and squashes, were their standard plantings, none of them at all demanding of attention or labor. They also grew cotton and tobacco and some fruit— pineapple and papaya in particular. With an abundance of fish, they were self-sufficient. A docile people, they were feudally organized under a cacique. They lived in small settlements close to fresh water, in simple houses, well roofed against the rains. Only hurricanes or droughts upset this equilibrium.

The selfsame crops are all flourishing in our *vecindad* at this moment. Pucho has a great spread of yucca growing just under the crest—a staple that feeds him year-round. Now we have additional staples—coconuts, bananas and plantains, rice, sugar, coffee, many more fruits—but the land and the fishing still provide practically all our food. Taino words are on our tongue every day—hammock, cassava, maize, tobacco, potato, canoe. Although the Taino population of Hispaniola was wiped out within thirty years of the discovery, it is as though the Tainos had left their mode of life embedded in the land, to be reenacted in a surprisingly similar form by the campesinos now. Rich soil, a benign climate, and plants of predictable yield guarantee basic survival, although today on a threadbare level. For the Tainos, however, it appears to have been an abundance, and their world was apparently both stable and peaceful. While the Tainos knew the whereabouts of gold, they made little use of it except for small ornaments. Sometimes, sitting on my terrace, I imagine what it must have been like for the Tainos, similarly perched, to see the caravels come into sight. Even today, when a boat of any size enters the bay we come out to gaze, as we do when a plane flies over.

In the letter Columbus wrote on the return crossing to Ferdinand and Isabella (it was addressed to Luis de Santangel, Crown Treasurer, for transmission to Their Catholic Majesties), he expanded on the nature of the Indians he had encountered, speaking of their timidity, their innocence, and the fact that they went unarmed and were both friendly to and fearful of the Spaniards—perfect material for conversion and for service to the Crown. He did report, however, that he had heard of an island peopled by warlike Indians, Caribs, who were known to eat human flesh, and who made sorties on the outlying islands. The details he gave of them—that they wore their hair long and carried bows and arrows—appear to have come from the confrontation and flash of force at Las Flechas. When his boat's crew told him of that encounter, he wrote of himself in the journal, on January 13, 1493, "In one way it troubled me, and in another way it did not, i.e., in that now they might be afraid of us. Without doubt, the people here are evil, and I believe they are from the Isle of Caribe, and that they eat men. . . . If these people are not Caribes, they must at least be inhabitants of lands fronting them and have the same customs, not like the others on the other islands who are without arms and cowardly beyond reason."

When the seventeen ships of the second voyage reached their destination in Hispaniola, with a company of about fifteen hundred, some domestic animals, and a variety of seeds, plants, and provisions, the long equilibrium that the Tainos had enjoyed ended. Columbus found the fort he had left destroyed, all the men dead—they had abused the Indians and had been overcome in turn. From this point on, Columbus never hesitated to show force in all his dealings with the Indians. They were to be subdued and turned to work in finding and extracting gold, before all else. The Spaniards as yet had no substantial permanent settlement, but they set out on expeditions to the interior, to track the gold. The course of subsequent events was perhaps set from the beginning by a fatal misunderstanding. On the first voyage, Columbus read from the gesticulations of the Indians he questioned that gold existed on the island in abundant quantities, and he reported that as fact. In truth, while gold did exist in the Cibao and in other alluvial placers, it was not widespread, plentiful, or easily accessible—certainly not to any degree that would satisfy the Admiral's by now burning expectations. Yet he continued to insist that it was, and drove the Indians more and more ferociously to produce it.

It did not take long to turn the feelings of the Tainos for the Spaniards from fear to hatred: they first rose against them in early 1494, and suffered fierce retribution. When a fleet of four ships left for Spain, in February of 1495, about five hundred Indian captives were aboard; nearly half of them died on the voyage. Columbus meanwhile set about crushing Indian resistance once and for all, which he did with a formidable force of men. He eventually secured the submission of most of the caciques, established a fort in the center of the island, and then decided on the site of the new capital, Santo Domingo—at the mouth of the Ozama River, in the south. From every Indian over fourteen the Admiral demanded a tribute of a small piece of gold every three months. The caciques begged to be released from the tribute of gold, offering instead to plant a vast stretch of land expressly for feeding the Spaniards, something to them of infinitely greater worth. But the Spaniards, fired by both greed and impatience, were unrelenting.

Failure to pay tribute resulted in increasingly brutal punishment— quite often, according to Las Casas, the cutting off of the Indians' hands—until, in 1497, orders came from Spain, in the form of Letters Patent, decreeing a *repartimiento*, a sharing out, of the colony. The plan was later modified to become one of granting the settlers *encomiendas*, tracts of land to use and cultivate, along with an Indian community to do each settler's bidding, with the understanding that the *encomendero* would in time convert his Indians to Christianity. The granting of *encomiendas*, however, was less about land than about Indians: in practice, a settler would be given a whole Indian community, under its cacique, to cultivate the land, to dig for gold, to do anything at all that the master might command. Religious instruction was not uppermost in the settlers' minds. By 1500, the enslavement of the Tainos was complete. The seven years of Columbus's governorship of Hispaniola had been chaotic for the Spaniards and disastrous for the Tainos. His authority over the Spanish settlers had frayed and eroded, and the revenues he had promised the Crown had not been realized. Orders came from Spain that he was to be replaced as governor by Francisco de Bobadilla; and when Bobadilla arrived in Santo Domingo, in August of 1500, his first act was to arrest Columbus and his two brothers, Bartholomew and Diego, and send them back to Spain in chains.

As for the Tainos, they were by now dwindling in number. Most of the detail that remains to us of that human erosion we owe to the extraordinarily observant and intelligent chronicle of Bartolomé de Las Casas. As a young man, in Seville, he had seen Columbus return in triumph from the first voyage in 1493, and his father and uncle had both preceded him to Hispaniola. He landed in Santo Domingo in 1502, and in his ten years there he was to bear witness to the steady extermination of the Tainos; in a growing state of moral outrage, he was led eventually to join the Dominican order and to dedicate his life to arguing the rights of the Indians and denouncing the brutalities of the conquest in his writings and in public debate in Spain. He often made his case in an eloquent polemic, but it is the details he patiently recorded in his history of the Indies which make his case for him now. He had a keen sense of the fatefulness of the times he was living in, and of the dangerous precedents being set. Were it not for him, we would know far less about the Tainos and their progressive destruction.

Among Las Casas' careful records we have his transcription of a sermon that the Dominican friar Antonio de Montesinos preached in Santo Domingo on the last Sunday of Advent, 1511, castigating the cruelty of the settlers and reminding them of their Christian obligations:

> Tell me, by what right or justice do you hold these Indians in such a cruel and horrible servitude? On what authority have you waged such detestable wars against these peoples, who dwelt quietly and peacefully on their own land? Wars in which you have destroyed such infinite numbers of them by homicides and slaughters never before heard of? Why do you keep them so oppressed and exhausted, without giving them enough to eat or curing them of the sicknesses they incur from the excessive labor you give them? And they die, or, rather, you kill them, in order to extract and acquire gold every day.
>
> And what care do you take that they should be instructed in religion, so that they may know their God and Creator, may be baptized, may hear Mass, and may keep Sundays and feast days? Are these not men? Do they not have rational souls? Are you not bound to love them as you love yourselves? Don't you understand this? Don't you feel this? Why are you sleeping in such a profound and lethargic slumber? Be assured that in your present state you can no more be saved than the Moors or Turks, who lack the faith of Jesus Christ and do not desire it.

Witnessing the massacre of Indians, Las Casas himself wrote, "Who of those born in future centuries will believe this? I myself who am writing this and saw it and know most about it can hardly believe that such was possible."

It may be that from the beginning the Tainos were doomed by the disturbance of their rural way of life. Their settlements were the known world to them; to be moved left them helpless. (The Spanish word *desalojamiento*, "to be turned out of home," is a word my neighbors always utter with a hush of horror.) Their finely balanced agricultural rhythm was broken. The domestic animals—cattle, pigs, horses—that the Spaniards had brought thrived on the vegetation and trampled free over cultivated land. The Tainos, besides, had no resistance of any kind—to European diseases, to the hard labor they were subjected to in the mines, to the demands and brutalities of the settlers, to the conditions of slavery, in Hispaniola or in Spain—and they died in vast numbers. The bitter cassava has a poisonous juice, which is squeezed out before making bread; the ubiquitousness of cassava meant that for the Tainos an easy means of suicide was at hand, and they used it liberally. A few fled—some, without doubt, to the Samaná Peninsula. An outbreak of smallpox in 1518 further reduced them. Most latter-day writers on the landings of the Spaniards concur in the opinion that what probably afflicted the Tainos more than anything else was the microbes and viruses introduced by the Spaniards. Las Casas estimated that some three million Tainos had died between 1494 and 1508, a figure now considered to be an exaggeration; but, as to the Taino population, there can be no definitive figures, only guesses. What is definitive is the fact that by the 1530s virtually no Tainos were left except a few hundred who had fled to Cuba and possibly a few who survived their slavery in Spain. As a people, they were extinct.

The letter Columbus wrote to Santangel for Their Majesties, with its glowing version of what he had discovered, was printed in Barcelona in 1493, and almost immediately translated into Latin. It sketches the Indians' way of life in a mode that carries echoes of Eden, Arcadia, and Columbus's own earlier fantasies. It caught the European imagination at once, this vision of unclothed, unarmed innocence, and it was to flower later in the writings of Montaigne, in the noble savage of Rousseau, and in other written utopias. It also gave the newly discovered lands an aura of promise and freedom that served as a spur to the many westward migrations from Europe that followed. With conquest, however, the Spanish view of the Indians changed quickly. The shift is visible in Columbus's own writings: the docile Tainos, friendly, eager to please, later become "cowards"; fear of the warlike Caribs takes precedence, a show of force is paramount. The native is animal, the paradise wilderness, both to be dominated and subdued. First seen as Ariel, the Indian is soon turned into Caliban: beast, slave, less than human.

The depletion of the Taino population left succeeding governors of Hispaniola with a serious lack of labor; new labor had to be found if the colony was to be of any further use to Spain. Hence, by 1518 African slaves were being brought to the island. They were stronger than the Tainos, better fitted for work in the mines and for cane cutting. Sugar had been introduced in 1515, and Hispaniola was turning from its exhausted gold-workings to agriculture. At the same time, however, Hispaniola was receding in importance to the Spanish Crown. In 1500 Alonso de Ojeda had discovered the coastline of what is now Colombia, with evidence of gold in quantity; and as news of that and of the later subjugation of Jamaica and Cuba, the excursions of Juan Ponce de León to Florida, in 1513, the further probing south by Vasco Núñez de Balboa, and Hernán Cortés's conquest of Mexico in 1519, filtered back steadily to Santo Domingo, many of the settlers determined to follow in these tracks, and abandon the colony for more immediate reward. To survive, if not to prosper, Hispaniola needed a settled population. Instead, Santo Domingo was becoming little more than a way station on the Spanish Main. The first Spaniards came less to colonize than to return home wealthy. The surge was westward. When López de Velasco came to write the official geography of the Indies, in 1574, he reported a population in Hispaniola of a thousand Spaniards, half of them in Santo Domingo, and thirteen thousand African Negroes, with large tracts of the island abandoned. The present population of the Dominican Republic is two-thirds mulatto, one-third divided between white and black. No one claims Taino blood.

Although Columbus has been mythified by history as the discoverer, he cannot be made to bear the blame for the greed and the brutality of those who came after him—men of a less visionary disposition. What set the ruthless tenor of the conquest, however, was the extravagant expectations that Columbus had created in his quest for patronage. His eagerness to confirm these expectations shows in what he chose to see on the first voyage. His later life seethed with frustration, as though he could never forgive the lands he had discovered for not giving him what they had promised, or what he had made them promise. His obsession with fulfilling the promise of abundant gold kept him from giving any thought to the territories he was meant to be governing, or maintaining any authority over the settlers. It was less the inhumanity of the settlers—although Las Casas has left us plenty of evidence of that—than the stupidity and mismanagement of the unfolding enterprise, coupled with the intrusion of disease, that made the Indians extinct in so short a time.

Living in Samaná off and on over these last years has without question made me Indian-minded in reading those chronicles. I find them horrifying. Whatever consequences the first voyage of Columbus may have had for the planet and for our present existence, I cannot see that the ensuing thirty years were other than a human disaster for Hispaniola, a record of cruel and pointless conquest that could have been otherwise. Pucho asks me a lot about the Tainos— I once read him from Las Casas the descriptions of their common crops and agricultural practices, and he was as startled as I was that everything was all still growing within shouting distance, that we were more or less enacting the Tainos' agricultural patterns, using their words, living more or less as they did except for our clothes and our discontents. Even though the Tainos were his precursors rather than his ancestors, even though his language and his religion come from the Spaniards, it is with the Indians, the victims, that he identifies. When I told Pucho earlier this year that sometime in 1992 three caravels would sail into Samaná Bay, past our beach, to anchor off Las Flechas, and some actor would come ashore in a Columbus suit, he was all for gathering a few picked men from the *vecindad* and taking the actor hostage, as a gesture.

Legends require simplification, and by the time Columbus became legend and statue he had been enshrined as the discoverer, in some sense the founder, of the New World, although this did not really happen until the nineteenth century. Nor was it entirely a Eurocentric view that gave him the name of discoverer—it appealed as much to North Americans to fix on the image of the Admiral's first, frail landfall as a legendary beginning. The discoverees are glossed over; the fate of the Tainos is hardly common knowledge. Plans for the quincentenary made clear that in the case of Columbus the clarification of history was giving way to its Disneyfication. The image of Columbus that loomed largest was the heroic one—in television series, in two feature films, in the gloss of magazine re-creation, and in the gush of highly colored simulation. A few years ago, an Italian film crew came to shoot part of a historical drama about Columbus on the north coast of Samaná. They used a group of villagers as extras, and left them somehow stranded in a time warp: they have never quite recovered from the experience, and talk of nothing else. In Samaná, we all felt like extras by the time the quincentenary had run its course.

By far the most imaginative suggestion I heard about an appropriate acknowledgment of the quincentenary was made on Dominican television by the Dominican economist and historian Bernardo Vega, just as President Balaguer was preparing to attend a summit meeting of Latin American and Iberian heads of state in Mexico. Vega urged him to advance the idea at the meeting that since the Club of Paris, an organization that keeps a supervisory eye on Third World debt, was already excusing the debts of some African countries, it should make the year 1992 memorable by wiping off the slate all the European debt accumulated by the countries of Latin America, as partial compensation for the wealth that had been extracted from that region, starting in 1492.

In the decade following Columbus's first landfall, the island of Hispaniola, for the Spaniards who descended on it, *was* the New World—its earliest incarnation. The first reports and chronicles also whetted the colonizing appetites of the other seafaring countries of Europe. As the conquistadores ventured farther and farther into the southern continent, establishing their maritime base at Cartagena, from which harbor the gold-bearing ships set out on the Spanish Main, a whole host of adventurers began to arrive on the scene, to take part in the general land grab in the Caribbean and to launch almost two centuries of piracy. In 1586, Sir Francis Drake occupied and sacked Santo Domingo. French buccaneers set up their harbors of operation on the island of Tortuga and on the north coast of Hispaniola, and on their sorties they also discovered the Samaná Peninsula, a natural hideout, well placed for raids on the gold lanes to the south. The remaining Spanish colonists could not muster sufficient strength to drive the French out. In 1697, they ceded the western part of the island altogether to France, and subsequently France peopled its new colony, Saint-Domingue, with bigger shipments of African slaves, to work in the increasingly lucrative sugar plantations. Spain's control of and interest in the colony waned considerably, and in 1795 it ceded the rest of the island to France. But, fired by news of the French Revolution, the slaves of Saint-Domingue began to rise in revolt, and, in 1804, succeeded in establishing the independent black republic of Haiti. Their revolutionary zeal and their determination to stamp out slavery led them into a series of aggressions against the rest of the island, and in 1822 a Haitian army occupied Santo Domingo and took over the whole island. It was the Haitian occupation that drove the colonists to unite in sufficient force to confront the invaders, to defeat them, and to declare, on February 27, 1844, the independent existence of the Dominican Republic.

The history of Hispaniola after Columbus—a history of factionalism, of foreign intrusions, of plot and counterplot—set a pattern that has continued into the island's turbulent present, and led to the republic's having had more than forty different governments between 1844 and 1916. It is a history that implies a deep division—a division between a few individuals with the ruthlessness to aspire to power and domination, on the one hand, and a quiescent people who have learned to survive whatever calamities break over their heads, on the other.

The Tainos were victims of the conquest, and, in a sense, those who have inhabited the farther reaches of the island have continued to be victims ever since. At no time was the colony free of foreign presence, of foreign domination, even after independence had been at least nominally achieved; and in this century it is the United States, rather than France or Spain, that now casts its long shadow over the island's affairs, to the point of direct intervention on two occasions. The United States Marines occupied the Dominican Republic from 1916 until 1924, when political chaos threatened civil war; and in 1965, on the same pretext, President Lyndon Johnson sent an occupying force to the island when street fighting in Santo Domingo threatened to spread and engulf the whole country. Between these two occupations came the long dictatorship of Rafael Leónidas Trujillo, who remained firmly in power from 1930 until 1961, ruling with such harsh authority that my neighbors still tend to lower their voices when they speak of his times.

I follow this history, and the history of Samaná in particular, with a kind of despairing fascination, for it reveals a pattern that I see persisting into the present—a kind of fatalistic acceptance. The Caudillo-Presidents of Dominican history—Pedro Santana, Buenaventura Baez, Ulises Heureaux—ruled as strongmen, like the caciques of old, and, in a way, laid the ground for Trujillo's absolute and unopposed rule over the country. They were his precursors. I quite often recount to Pucho what I have been reading, but it surprises him not at all, for he remembers the days of Trujillo, and finds none of the brutalities of Dominican history difficult to believe. Like all Dominicans who were alive at the time, he remembers exactly where he was when the rumor spread that El Chivo was dead. "We did not dare to believe it at first, so we all went indoors and whispered," he told me once. "We stayed up all night, wondering. And then, the next morning, when the news was sure, we all went out, every single person in the village I lived in, and walked about and talked the whole day. Nobody thought about working. But we talked in whispers, because we were still afraid."

Thirty years dead, Trujillo still mesmerizes Dominicans. In conversations he comes up all the time. "*Cuando Trujillo*"—"in Trujillo's day"—I hear someone say, and a story will follow, of a horror, most likely, but always recounted with an edge of awe in the teller's voice. Any impending disaster—a gasoline shortage, a dearth of cement, a national strike—will cause Trujillo to be evoked: what my neighbors most fear is chaos and breakdown, and what he stamped on the country during his long rule was an unbreakable order, an authoritarian predictability. He lasted longer than any of the tyrants who preceded him, he amassed more power, property, and personal wealth, he made the military into a personal force for control, he dispensed patronage and punishment with such remorseless cunning as to paralyze his countrymen, and yet he still is remembered by a good many Dominicans as a stern father, who would take care of every eventuality, whose whims were law, but who would save them from chaos.

The mold in which Trujillo cast Dominican society has not been broken. In many ways, the country under Trujillo resembled the Hispaniola of colonial days: a feudal society with a governing elite and a large, docile peasantry. The two-thirds of the people who lived in rural areas accepted both their poverty and their powerlessness. Crime was punished mercilessly, as was opposition in any form. Life was predictable, and accepted with a fatalism that I still encounter every day. "*Somos infelices*," the rural Dominicans say very often, meaning "It is our destiny to be poor." At the other extreme lies the capital—Ciudad Trujillo in the dictator's day, Santo Domingo now—where military, fiscal, and commercial power is concentrated, where fortunes, deals, and decisions are made, where favors are

78

peddled. In his heyday, Trujillo was estimated to be one of the richest men in the world; he instituted a form of state capitalism in which he was the state. The identification of political power with self-enrichment is fixed forever in the popular mind, and, indeed, it has hardly been disproved by the elected governments of the last thirty years.

Trujillo's death left the country floundering in uncertainties. It had no institutional structure to maintain it. Pressures from the United States, which feared then that the Cuban Revolution might spread to the Dominican Republic, led to the holding of democratic elections in December of 1962. Although Dominicans had only a sketchy understanding of what democracy meant, they elected a populist President, Juan Bosch, who promised sweeping social reforms and political freedom, even to the Communists. Those promises proved too much for the elite and the military, and nine months later Bosch was overthrown and exiled in a military coup. A junta ruled uneasily for eighteen months, until the constitutionalists rose in a popular surge against the military; they seemed almost on the point of defeating it when Lyndon Johnson ordered in the Marines, to quench what was the closest to a revolution that the people of the country had ever come. Elections were held again in 1966, and have been held every four years since.

My neighbors remain distrustful of democracy as they know it. A change of party in Samaná means a change of all official posts in the town, from governor to itinerant mailman, but apart from that the campesinos see little or no improvement in their lot. Some, embittered by the lack of opportunity and of paid work, turn their eyes elsewhere, but the majority fall back on the ingrained pattern, the preoccupation with finding food every day. Only the luck of the climate and the bounty of the soil have kept them from misery. As for democracy, their participation ends with the elections, for Dominican Presidents do not govern so much as rule by decree. In Samaná, the pattern still has not changed. We live at the end of the line, the receiving end of whatever may come from the capital—government decrees, price rises, shortages, delays—and everything makes us wary of life outside the peninsula. Although all my neighbors vote proudly on Election Day, dipping their index fingers in indelible ink to make sure they vote no more than once, they do not expect anything to change. They all tell stories of electoral frauds, vote buying, false counts, as though to insulate themselves against disappointment.

Although the Dominican Republic shares Hispaniola with Haiti, the landmass is virtually all that they do share. Dominicans harbor a deep prejudice against Haitians, an inherent racism that is seldom voiced but is pervasively present. It stems in part from the violence of their history—Dominicans never forget that it was from Haiti that they wrested their independence. And now that their country is considerably more developed than its threadbare neighbor, with a much higher per capita income, they do not welcome those Haitians who filter across the frontier, except as braceros, cane-cutters who work in conditions not far removed from slavery—a circumstance that has brought the Dominican Republic the censure of the United Nations Commission on Human Rights.

Of the many cruelties perpetrated by Trujillo, the most barbaric of all took place in October of 1937, when units of the Dominican Army, acting on a direct order from the dictator, hunted down and massacred between 15,000 and 20,000 Haitians—men, women, and children—in the Dominican provinces adjoining the frontier. The event was covered up at the time, and today Dominicans go silent when it is mentioned.

The border between the two countries is tightly closed, vaster than geography. Given the present doleful situation in Haiti, it might occur to any outsider that the simplest solution would be for the Dominican government to open temporary refugee camps in its territory; but, with Dominican attitudes as unyielding as they are, it's not surprising that Haitians in their despair choose to chance the open sea rather than look toward the forbidding frontier to the east.

Dr. Joaquín Balaguer began his political career in the thirties, as a loyal servant of Trujillo, in a variety of official posts and eventually as Trujillo's puppet President—the post he occupied when Trujillo was assassinated. Balaguer's image could not be more different from that of his master—he is small, meek of manner, frail, soft-spoken, well known as a poet, scholar, and historian—yet, unscrupulous and politically astute, he has never strayed far from the exercise of power. He won the elections of 1966, which followed the American intervention, and governed steadily until 1978—a period in which the country enjoyed a brief prosperity, thanks to a surge in sugar prices—and he returned to power in 1986, at the age of seventy-nine, and was reelected in a dubious election in 1990. He is now blind, yet his hold on power has been as tenacious as ever Trujillo's was, his mode of governing as autocratic, his use of patronage in government appointments as cunning, his command of the military as secure. He has used propaganda zealously, seeking to appear in the role of a benign grandfather who has given his entire life to his country. Yet nowadays, the length and breadth of the country, on the minibuses and in the market, you hear no good words for Balaguer—not even from those who voted for him. When I was last in the capital, you could read the same legend scrawled on corner after corner: "*Que se vaya ya!*"—"Let him leave now!" And what brought discontent to a head was, as much as anything, the quincentenary.

When Balaguer was returned to office in 1986, he launched a vast program of public building, mostly in the capital—construction projects that had a great deal to do with the appearance of the place and bore his name more often than not. It was as though Balaguer, in his last years in power, were bent on fulfilling in new concrete Trujillo's obsession with public self-enshrinement. He also had firmly in mind a project he was determined to carry through: the building of a huge lighthouse, the Faro a Colón, to commemorate Columbus's landing in 1492.

The idea of a lighthouse as a monument to Columbus's arrival was first put forth in the middle of the last century, and it stayed alive until, at the Fifth International American Conference, held in Santiago, Chile, in 1923, a resolution was passed to build such a lighthouse monument on the edge of Santo Domingo "with the co-operation of the governments and peoples of America." In 1929, an international competition was announced, with a prize of $10,000, for the design of such a shrine. The entries were sifted by a special commission, and in 1931 an international jury met in Madrid to study 455 submissions, from forty-eight countries. The award went, finally, to a young English architect, J. L. Gleave, who was still a student, and artists' impressions of his design for the Faro appeared in the Dominican press of the day. Time passed; then Trujillo took up the idea of the Faro with characteristic grandiloquence, planning a complex of buildings around the lighthouse, including a new Presidential palace for himself, and actually breaking ground for the project in April of 1948. The money promised by the other governments of Latin America was not forthcoming, however, and the Faro remained merely a plan. For Balaguer, however, the building of the Faro remained, from the years of the competition on, a matter of deep commitment: it was his destiny to build it, to bring it to completion. He bided his time, and in 1986 work on the Faro began in earnest. The quincentenary was six years away. There was no time to lose.

Over these past few years, I watched the Columbus Lighthouse lumber into being in the Parque del Este, on the east side of the Ozama River, looking across to the Colonial Quarter of Santo Domingo, and to the cathedral, where the lead casket with Columbus's remains lay, before being transferred to the finished lighthouse. At first, a forced clearing of the area around the site dismantled the shanty-towns and drove out about fifty thousand people, many of whom were given no promise of rehousing. On the bare, muddy expanse left by the bulldozers, the Faro began to rise.

We think of lighthouses as vertical towers that project a light horizontally, for ships to see. The Columbus Lighthouse, however, is a horizontal structure, like a recumbent beast, designed to throw its light vertically, upward. It has a long base and two stubby arms—the shape of a long cross or a short sword. Since it was clearly intended as one of the new wonders of the world, its scale is immense: it is nearly half a mile long; walls slant upward from each arm to meet at a point a hundred and twenty feet high, and are crowned with a beacon that is to project on the sky a lighted cross visible as far away as Puerto Rico, some two hundred miles east. It has the look of a concrete pyramid with one long extended arm: a humped, dinosaur look; an anonymous, inert grayness. Grass has now grown over the razed barrios, along with newly planted stands of trees bordering a web of new approach roads. At first sight, it has a curious effect on the eye, puzzling rather than impressive, and seems mournful and forbidding. You could easily believe that some huge, unnameable secret weapon was being assembled deep inside it. It puts me in mind more of Dr. No than of Columbus.

Since Balaguer resumed the Presidency in August of 1990, things have been going very badly in the Dominican Republic. The elections were held that May, and we listened avidly to the first returns on the radio—the neighbors excitedly, for Juan Bosch appeared to be leading Balaguer. Suddenly, however, the electoral count was suspended, incomplete—nobody understood quite why. After a tense day or two, we were all back at work, while in the capital a bitter wrangling began. It lasted weeks, and finally, in mid-June, the electoral junta announced that Balaguer had won. Even so, the combined opposition votes exceeded his by half a million, making him very much a minority President. No one doubted that there had been electoral fraud. I knew of some in Samaná. Electoral fraud is not easy to bring off in our present political climate; for having done it, Balaguer did elicit some admiration. Those who had hoped that he might abandon his construction projects and give some attention to the backward state of the country's agriculture—which is to say, to the bare livelihood of those who lived outside the capital—were soon disenchanted; one of his first acts was to set in motion plans for the rapid completion of the Faro a Colón. That year was a drastic one for the campesinos, first in soaring prices of basic foods, and then in serious shortages of fuel and, of all things, sugar. The price of gasoline rose, and rose again. Perhaps even worse was the precarious state of the country's electrical grid, which occasioned nationwide daily electricity cuts, sometimes of twenty hours—cuts that played havoc with refrigeration, and with commerce in general. If there was hunger in the countryside, there was misery in the slums on the edges of the capital. Balaguer continued in Olympian indifference, unperturbed, deaf to dissent.

The ironies surrounding Balaguer's obsession with the Faro were ever more apparent. How much had the Faro cost to build? Twenty million dollars? A hundred million? People guess, but nobody will ever know, since Balaguer does not make public such accountings. Its light was to be the brightest in all the Americas, a stunning irony in a country whose electrical system is all but bankrupt. When the Faro is switched on, the campesinos said, the lights will go out in all the rest of the country. Besides, they remind you, sailors have no need of lighthouses anymore. And, they added, when he switched on the Faro, poor Balaguer wouldn't even be able to see the light.

I eavesdrop a lot on the long bus trips to Samaná, and in 1992 the general talk always came around to the Faro, for it became, understandably, the incarnation of discontents, an object of concentrated scorn among the campesinos. At times, you heard the fervently expressed hope that when Balaguer pressed the button to switch on the Faro he would somehow be subsumed into it and projected skyward, and, with him, all politicians, to join Columbus in his Faro, because they've been doing to us the very thing that he did, haven't they, with rice now at five pesos a pound. It was not rage, however, that they directed toward the Faro—Dominicans, as they tell me often, are not good haters. They are too good-natured. Instead, they made the Faro into a national joke, a monument to absurdity—not just the absurdity of their own situation but the absurdity of all such monumentalizing, at a time when the world is more bent on tearing down shrines to the past than on building them. The five hundred years that the Faro was enshrining represented for the campesinos a very different history from that promulgated in the official publications of the quincentenary commission in Santo Domingo.

As it turned out, the inauguration of the Faro did not exactly fulfill Balaguer's lifelong dream; instead, it engendered a new respect for the *fucú* throughout the country. The world leaders who had been invited to attend the ceremony sent their excuses, to a man; the Pope, who was in the Dominican Republic to attend an ecumenical congress, pointedly absented himself. More poignantly, however, Balaguer's sister, his long companion, died the day before the event, and he himself could not be present. Although the Faro sends its light skyward at appointed hours, visitors mostly ignore it, and the people take the only revenge that is in their power by never mentioning it, by effectively forgetting its existence.

Balaguer's other interest in his policy of Dominican glorification has been, inevitably, tourism, and in the late eighties, especially, the country has seen a rash of hotel building and resort-making along the Caribbean coast, in the south, and on the wilder, Atlantic north coast, bringing with it all the furniture of tourist occupation, and all the expectations. It appears at first a very simple and agreeable proposition to those who live there: tourists come with money, and wish to stay, and so one must offer them something that will cause them to hand over some, if not all, of their money. It appeals to the young in the *aldeas* who have other ideas than trudging back and forth from the *conucos* all their lives. And it appealed enough to the first tourists so that the Dominican Republic has been turned into a kind of modern discovery, worthy of being called unspoiled.

Not for long, however. Already, two towns on the north coast have been overtaken by mass tourism and turned quickly into overcrowded, traffic-ridden nightmares. Huge projects, some of them bearing Columbus's name, have started up, foundered, and failed, leaving monumental arched gateways leading to wilderness. Restaurants open in hope and quite often close in disappointment. There is work, of course, in construction—"building bars we can't afford to go into," as Orlando, the mason, likes to remark. We talk about tourism a lot by the stream, most seriously whenever there is a question of selling land. For a campesino to sell his land would mean money in the hand, something never known. But would the money in the hand last as the land lasts? In reality, the coming of tourism has made very little difference to the life of our *vecindad*, except for the occasional work it has offered in construction. It has, however, brought with it a great deal of *ilusión*, high hopes, great expectations.

Porfirio, who has a house above mine, by the road, a favorite meeting place in the neighborhood, got a job as a foreman, building a small hotel in town—a good job, which gave him, after a year, enough to leave it and buy a black-and-white television set, and an automobile battery, which is recharged once a week. Every night now, the blue light flickers in Porfirio's house after sundown, and of an evening there will be thirty neighbors cross-legged in rows, transfixed but still talkative, with sleeping children among them. Sometimes I have gone up to see Porfirio and sat for a while, listening to the audience reaction. No matter what soap is sobbing its crisis on the screen, they are giving the drama only minimal attention. They point out the clothes, they crow at the food, they ogle the cars, they embrace the commercials. They are gazing through a window at a world they instantly want, and tourists are to them somehow emissaries from that world.

The inevitable discontents that are fueled by the coming of tourists have led a lot of country people to leave behind them a life that, predictable though it is, gets harder rather than easier and holds out no hope of anything else. They may go to the capital, where they find that unemployment is chronic, prices are high, survival is much more precarious. Or they may take a more drastic course. In Samaná sometimes, on moonless nights, we will hear a boat pass, a boat of some power, but without lights. It is a *yola*, most likely—an open boat setting out with perhaps twenty people who have paid over most of their savings to the boatmaster to take them across the dangerous waters of the Mona Channel and land them, illegally, on a beach on

85

the west shore of Puerto Rico. Some of the boats come to grief, and the sharks turn crossings into tragedies. Of those who land, some are caught at once, some later; but a good many filter in, an address in a pocket, are looked after at first by other Dominicans, then find work, hoping in time to send some money home and to save enough to make the flight to New York, untroubled by immigration, armed with more addresses, to find better work, eventually to become legal, with the dream of saving enough to set up a small *colmado* back in the *vecindad* they began in. One of the men from our neighborhood went in a *yola*, worked in Puerto Rico for three months, was caught, and was returned by plane, his first flight. The fine he had to pay consumed all the money he had saved. We all turned out to welcome him back, however, and he has become something of a counsellor to others with *yolas* in mind. A nurse I know in town went in a *yola*, which was stopped about a mile out by the Dominican coast guard and turned back, the money confiscated (and later shared with the captain of the *yola*, she was sure). Every time I return to Samaná, there is an absence, a space: someone I know has gone in a *yola*.

In the Dominican Republic, Christmas and Easter are marked by the return, in flocks, of *Dominicanos ausentes*—those who live in the United States—on a visit to their pueblos, bearing gifts, wearing the gold chains and bright new clothes of success, and full of stories of color and light, even if the chains, and possibly the roll of bills, have been borrowed for the occasion. The myth is perpetuated. I have spent considerable time explaining some of the complexities of that other world to my neighbors—things like paying for heat, which is incomprehensible to them. But it is a world they have come to want fiercely, even if only in the form of sneakers—simply, a better life. Over the last twenty years, there has been a Dominican diaspora that has taken almost a million out of the country.

I am by now used to the fatalism of my neighbors. It is a cheerful fatalism rather than a despairing one, mostly, although hopes and expectations are scarce. I know a good number of Dominicans, however, who are acutely aware of the situation in their country and have a clear view indeed of a possible future for it. Among them is a farmer, Gilberto, with whom I often talk, for he experiments indefatigably with new seeds that I bring him. I asked him last summer what he would like to see happen in his country.

He did not hesitate for a second. "More than anything, I wish this country would lose its memory," he said. "We're still slaves of our own history—what happened to us is what we still expect to happen. I long to see the age of the *abuelos*, the grandfathers, Balaguer and Bosch, come to an end. Over thirty years, they have made it harder for those who live in the campo, never worse than now. I'd like to wipe out our present parties and politicians, all the corruption and patronage and secret deals, all the intrigue. I'd like to see an end to this weakness we have of always looking for a leader, a father—a grandfather, even—who will save us, who will make all our decisions for us, whom we can curse and grumble at. Our parties don't have programs. All they do is parade their candidate for savior, hoping enough of us will say, 'That's the man!' We need parties that put forward programs, not saviors. We need young technocrats in the government who can come up with a national plan that will open up the country, give it work, and, most of all, *involve* us in our own country, give us some hope. I'd like to see all our children literate, our teachers and doctors paid decent salaries, the police, too, so that they didn't have to turn to crime. If only we modernized our agriculture, if we diversified from our sugar dependence, we could be the garden state of the Caribbean. We wouldn't need tourism to save us. Tourism is another kind of slavery for Dominicans. Spaniards call tourism *putería*—whoring—and that's what it is, pleasing foreigners. It's corrupting, it's like a pollution. Take Samaná. If the government gave Samaná a million dollars for agricultural projects, well supervised, we could be exporting fruit and vegetables year-round, to other islands, to Florida, and living well. We could have solar energy and irrigation systems and crops year-round. Instead, they talk of a golf course. Can you imagine what an insult it is to us, who have always lived from the land, to put down a golf course among us? Or to build that monstrous monument to Columbus? As far as I'm concerned, Columbus didn't so much discover America as bring into being the Third World."

Samaná, at the end of the line, has always had a trickle of tourists, but its facilities are still frail and few. The place survives, however, on rumors of imminent prosperity; and while many of its projects have foundered, some are coming to fruition. At the moment, the place lives in a kind of limbo of possibilities, and the *chisme* this year has been a little headier than usual. The mayor of Miami made a visit, in 1991, expressed his undying love for Samaná, and promised to send

87

a consignment of used official cars from Miami, which have so far not arrived. A group of conservationists has been taking a growing interest in Samaná for the last three years, and a plan is afoot to have the bay and the peninsula declared a Biosphere Reserve, to maintain the native species, including the manatee, to prevent pollution of the bay, and to protect the habitat of the humpback whales that spend their breeding time in the bay from late January until early March every year, before their migration north. It has not been easy for me to explain to the neighbors just what a Biosphere Reserve means, or would mean to them. They are mystified by the notion; I think they see themselves as having to dress up as Tainos.

Most of the *chisme*, however, surrounded the opening of a luxury hotel, on an outcrop of rocky coast overlooking the beach at Las Flechas and facing the little island of Cayo Levantado. The hotel took shape in fits and starts for three years, and a number of men from our neighborhood worked on it at various times. It is built in James Bond Caribbean: red roofs, verandas, palms wild and potted, a private force of uniformed guards, and a tariff that, if the *chisme* is close, sets everyone's eyes rolling. About a quarter of a mile from the hotel sits the small town of Los Cacaos, hugging the beach and sprawling up the slope—a jaunty, easygoing, raucous community of people, who are quite fired up by the sudden transformation of their coast. If any one of the inhabitants of Los Cacaos had in hand what a guest pays to sleep a night in the hotel, he would instantly be among the richest in town. Tourists, as a rule, want to go shopping; and shopping in the town of Samaná offers the slimmest of pickings. There is the market, where goats' throats are often cut in public; there is a hardware store like an Aladdin's cave; there are venders of hats made of varnished palm leaves; and there are three shoeshine boys who stare gloomily at tourist sandals. But there is not much more except for the roar of motorcycles, the main attainable dream of young Dominicans. I cannot think that much good can come from placing two such disparate groups, so far apart economically, in such sudden proximity. At best, they trouble each other; and certainly the hotel's presence feeds local discontents, when people at scarcely survival level live in such an opulent shadow. They fear that very soon their own beaches will be closed to them, as has begun to happen, and, worse, that they may be forced to move—to yield up their land to the needs of tourism—by government decree. The tourist enterprises that have been successful in the Dominican Republic are those in which the tourists are enclosed in vast, caged, patrolled compounds, the concentration camps of leisure, with Dominican workers shipped in during the day and out at night. The fence makes sense. The division is dire. Besides, after the first flush of construction tourism does not bring the abundance of work it initially seems to promise. The revenues do not filter down in any noticeable way to the local inhabitants. I would not be surprised to see some local merry men form a latter-day Robin Hood band, swooping down from the palm trees and turning Samaná into a tropical version of Sherwood Forest.

Simultaneously, however, another future hovers over Samaná. In October of 1990, the Dominican government signed an agreement with an American-owned company called Once Once, S.A., granting it the right to explore for oil in certain parts of the country, among them Samaná Bay. While it is difficult to see how the place might become a tourist mecca, a Biosphere Reserve, and a center for oil exploration all at once, such considerations are of little concern to Balaguer, who will not be around to face the consequences. Nor do my neighbors show much alarm or consternation at these prospects. Whatever may come to pass, it will happen to them as it happened to the Tainos, without any regard for their preferences; it has become their nature to accept rather than want. They gaze at the cruise ships that nose into Samaná Bay with the same wary eyes, the same unease, with which the Indians watched the coming of the caravels.

Columbus's first voyage is by now a matter more of legend than of history; but two scholars, Dr. J. L. Montalvo Guenard, in a thesis published in Puerto Rico in 1933, and the Dominican historian Bernardo Vega, in a recent paper, have, from a close reading of the text of the journal, made a strong case for Columbus's Samaná landfall taking place not on the beach of Las Flechas but at Rincón, at the far end of the peninsula. They have convinced me; but it is unlikely that the history books will be revised. I tried to explain this quibble to Pucho, but he only looked at me with a mixture of scorn and alarm that I could find nothing better to do with my time. The idea that the new hotel may be founded on a historical misplacement tickles him, however.

It seems to me salutary that some serious arguments over Columbus and the Spanish Conquest arose as they did at this precise stage in our global history, since they raise disturbing questions about the meanings and evaluations of the past—questions that matter not to historians alone. We live in a postcolonial world, and we have, in our time, grown steadily more adamant about human rights, more sensitive to their violation. It seems to me that this must inevitably affect our reading and reassessment of history. It is why we gravitate to seeing the conquest through the eyes of Las Casas rather than those of Columbus, and why we are grateful for his clarity, his humanity, and his indignation. We may argue about human rights, for they are, in a sense, abstractions, but we do not argue about human wrongs. We recognize them physically; we can point to them, in the past as in the present. Shame and indignation are our measures, as they were to Las Casas. Confronting human wrongs is our common cause at present. About the wrongs of the past we can do nothing, but we can at least look at them squarely, and see them clearly.

Basilisks' Eggs

B E I N G A N occasional translator, more by accident than by design, I feel somewhat rueful about the whole question of translating between languages. Its mysterious nature can become something of an obsession, for each act of translation is an unprecedented exercise; yet it is an obsession shared by a minority of people who live and read in more than one language, or whose work requires them to function simultaneously on different linguistic planes—spies, displaced persons, the Swiss, international soccer referees, interpreters, travel guides, anthropologists, and explorers. Translators enjoy the status, more or less, of literary mechanics, reassembling texts from one language to function in another; and even if they do more than that, their work is likely to get little more than a passing nod, if it is mentioned at all—understandably, for there can be only a very small body of readers capable of passing judgment on translations, and most of us are glad to have them at all. Translators require the self-effacing disposition of saints; and, since a good translation is one in which a work appears to have been written and conceived in the language into which it is translated, good translators grow used to going unrewarded and unnoticed, except by a sharp-nosed troop of donnish reviewers (we call them "the translation police") who seem to spend their reading lives on the lookout for errors.

As far as translations go, the English language is well served. Its great range makes it capable of accommodating Indo-European languages quite comfortably, and in recent years our book thirst has given rise to a steady flow of translation, discovering other literatures and giving foreign classics a new lease on life. I remember once checking up in Spain to see which English-language writers were most translated into Spanish, and being astonished to find complete, leather-bound sets of Somerset Maugham and Zane Grey leading the field. The translation barrier is a chancy one, and not everything that crosses it arrives in the best of condition. Vladimir Nabokov once remarked (as few but he are in a position to remark) that while a badly written book is a blunder, a bad translation is a crime. It has occurred to me at times that the translation police might well be given statutory powers to revoke the licenses of unreliable translators, as a service to language.

It is one thing to read a book in translation; it is quite another to *read* a translation, for that requires two languages, two texts, and an attention hovering between them. Such close reading of translations has something in common with solving word puzzles, perhaps, but it can prove extraordinarily revealing about the nature of the two languages—about the nature of language itself. Just as knowing more than one language shatters the likelihood of confusing word and thing, so reading the same work in more than one language draws attention to it as a literary construct—gives the work an added dimension, which may or may not enhance it.

It also draws attention to quite another quality of literature— namely, its translatability or untranslatability. Straightforward linear prose can usually pass without much effort into other languages; but there are some works of literature whose verbal complexity appears to doom them to remain in their own language. Lyric poetry, where compression of meaning is most intense, and in which the sound pattern forms part of the total meaning, comes high on the list of untranslatables—Rilke would be a good example—and yet this does not prevent odd felicities of translation at the hands of poets, or even variant translations of the same poem. It is precisely those works that seem by their linguistic intricacy to be untranslatable that often generate real brilliance in a translator. If anyone doubts that pleasure can come from translation, let him look, for instance, at Henri Bué's 1869 version of *Alice in Wonderland* in French, in which even the puns are rendered by equivalent puns, or Barbara Wright's versions of Raymond Queneau, or the Gardner-Levine rendering, with the author's help, of Guillermo Cabrera Infante's *Tres Tristes Tigres*— works in which wordplay apparently indigenous to another language is matched in English. For a translator, untranslatability can be as much a lure as a deterrent.

I keep pinned on my wall a remark made in an interview by

Octavio Paz: "Every translation is a metaphor of the poem trans-
lated," he says. "In this sense, the phrase 'poetry is untranslatable'
is the exact equivalent of the phrase 'all poetry is translatable.' The
only possible translation is poetic transmutation, or metaphor. But I
would also say that in writing an original poem, we are translating
the world, transmuting it. Everything we do is translation, and all
translations are in a way creations."

Translation has always been more haphazard than systematic, de-
pending on the enthusiasm of publishers and the dedication of indi-
vidual translators. André Gide used to maintain that every writer
owed it to his own language to translate at least one foreign work
to which his talents and temperament were suited, and there is no
question that translation has become a more serious and system-
atic endeavor. The most admirably concerted effort of translation
into English in recent years has been the rendering by various hands
of the new writing from Latin America—probably the most ener-
getic and inventive body of literature, particularly where the novel
is concerned, in present-day writing. Its reputation preceded it into
English—a perfect recipe for disappointment—but by now its main
works have appeared in English and continue to appear with mini-
mal delay, so that rumor has been given fairly immediate substance,
and readers are able to experience it in its impressive diversity. It is
a literature with a surprisingly recent momentum. The Uruguayan
critic Emir Rodríguez Monegal puts his finger on the year 1940—the
year the South American continent became culturally isolated as a
result of the Spanish Civil War and, on its heels, the Second World
War, and was driven into a preoccupation with its own national iden-
tities. From that time on, a reading public has been mushrooming
in Latin America, and writers have been virtually summoned into
being. It seems a long time since the Great American Novel has even
been contemplated in the United States; but Latin American novel-
ists seem to have their sights set on nothing less. The continent has
dawned on them as unwritten history, untapped literary resource—
the indigenous Indians, the Spanish Conquest, the stirrings of inde-
pendence, the subsequent tyrannies, the bizarre immigrations, the
economic colonization from Europe and the North, the racial confu-
sions, the paradoxes of national character, the Cuban revolution and
military oppressions, the great sprawl and struggle of the present.

There exists in Latin America now such enthusiasm about literature that writers are attended to like rock stars. What is more, the writers all read one another, know one another, review one another, and are refreshingly pleased at one another's existence, as though they felt themselves part of a huge literary adventure, a creative rampage. They are enviously placed in time, for part of their literary experience has been to read all the diverse experiments that have taken place in other literatures in the course of this century—experiments of which they have been avid students but not imitators, for their own writing is hugely inventive and varied in its manner.

Just as it would be practically impossible to discover anything like a unified culture in as sprawling a context as Latin America, so it is unfeasible to find or create a common language, for in the hundred and fifty years since the majority of the Latin American countries gained their independence from Spain the language has been steadily diversifying—separating itself from Castilian Spanish much as American English did from English English, breeding varieties of urban slang, breaking up in many directions—so that writers in search of a new realism seemed doomed instead to an inevitable regionalism. It is to Jorge Luis Borges that Latin American writers owe one powerful and influential solution to this dilemma, for Borges wrote in a language of his own—a highly literary language, unlike language in currency, a language that draws attention to itself, mocks itself, casts suspicion on itself. From Borges came the beguiling reminder that language is a trick, a manipulation of reality rather than a reflection of it—a notion that stems, after all, from Cervantes. His economy, his playful erudition, his ironies, his treatment of rational knowledge and language as fantastic games dazzled not only Latin Americans but also, in the first translations of his work, a whole crop of American and European writers. He has been both source and challenge, especially to the younger writers, for, although repudiating his archconservatism, they have taken a cue from him in looking for the concomitantly appropriate language for their own fantastic realities.

*

The two writers who have dominated the literary scene in Latin America are Borges and the Chilean poet Pablo Neruda, who died in late 1973. What is most curious about their coexistence is how little they have to do with each other as writers, how seldom they met or even mentioned each other as men, how drastically different their work is, and yet how Latin American each is, in his separate way. Borges's collected work is as sparse and spare as Neruda's is abundant and ebullient, metaphysical as Neruda's is free-flowing, dubious as Neruda's is passionately affirmative or condemnatory. Where Neruda is open and even naïve, Borges is subtle and skeptical; where Neruda is a sensualist, Borges is an ascetic; where Neruda writes of tangible, physical experience, Borges's fund of experience is purely literary—he looks on reading as a form of time travel. Although Borges roots his stories in Buenos Aires, Latin America is for him something of a metaphor, a geographical fiction. Neruda, quite to the contrary, celebrates, in hymnic joy or rage, the inexhaustible particularity of the Latin American continent. For him, language is largesse, and his human concern made his political commitment inevitable.

The lives and careers of these two writers have diverged as widely as their work. Borges, suffering from a gradual congenital blindness, lived from his earliest years *within* books and language, fascinated by stories of his soldiering ancestors and of the celebrated knife-fighters of Buenos Aires. What probably distinguishes him most as a writer is the profoundly disquieting effect he has on his readers. However remote and literary his subject matter may appear, he makes the experience of paradox so tangible and eerie that it persists almost as a spell—if after reading Borges one were, say, to miss a train, the event would be dressed in ominous significance. What Borges helped to do for Latin American writing was to rescue it from the slough of naturalism into which it had fallen and make it once again the province of the individual imagination; but he remains a difficult master in his sheer inimitability. Neruda has proved to be an influence more to the taste of present-day Latin American writers, if a less directly technical one. His output was prodigious, a progression in which he shed poetic selves like skins, moving from an early wild surrealism in the direction of human engagement and political commitment, never losing his vision but deliberately simplifying his language. It was a lesson in turning literature to account that was not lost on the younger writers, who for the most part see themselves as similarly engaged. Neruda himself, after a long diplomatic career, served as President Salvador Allende's Ambassador to Paris from 1971 until 1973, and died in Chile twelve days after the coup of September 1973—a death that inevitably became symbolic. It is the intensity and scale of his commitment to Latin America that keep him an important figure for the writers who have come after him.

For some years now, I have been translating poems of both Borges and Neruda, coming to know both men well and their work even better, for one never enters the being of a poem as completely as when one is translating it. It is an odd exercise of spirit, to enter another imagination in another language and then to try to make the movement of it happen in English. Untranslatability that no ingenuity can solve does arise, which is to say that some poems *are* untranslatable. (I keep a notebook of these untranslatables, for they are small mysteries, clues to the intricate nature of a language.) To a translator, Borges and Neruda are exigent in different ways. Borges learned English as a child, read voraciously in English, and has been influenced in the formal sense more by English writing— Stevenson, Kipling, Chesterton, Anglo-Saxon poetry, and the English poetic tradition—than by Spanish literature. In his stories, he tends to use English syntactical forms and prose order—making his Spanish curiously stark but easily accessible to English translation. Indeed, translating Borges into English often feels like restoring the work to its natural language, or retranslating it. In his poems, Borges leans heavily on English verse forms and on many of the formal mannerisms of English poetry, so that translating his poems calls for technical ingenuity and prosodic fluency, precision being all-important. His poems are so thoroughly objectified, however, that no great leaps of interpretation have to be made in translating them. It requires only the patience to refine and refine, closer and closer to the original. Neruda's poems present absorbingly different problems, though not just in their extravagance of language, their hugely varying themes and forms; what distinguishes them is their special tone, an intimacy with the physical world, the ability to enter and become things. (Neruda was commonly referred to in the conversation of his friends as *el vate*, the seer.) To translate his poems requires one to enter them and wear them, on the way to finding a similar tone in English.

Neruda's larger poems have a vatic intensity that is difficult to con-
tain in credible English, and has its closest affinities with Whitman,
an engraving of whom always sat on his writing table. But his more
personal lyrics are within closer reach of English, and, given linguis-
tic luck, are not unre-creatable. Translation is a mysterious alchemy
in the first place; but it becomes even more so in the experience of
entering the language and perception of two writers who have read
human experience so differently and have worded it in such distinct
ways—of becoming both of them, however temporarily.

It is interesting to compare the fate of these two writers in trans-
lation. Borges has earned such attention in English, and the body
of his work is so comparatively small, that translating him in his
entirety is a feasible project. (This has not been entirely to Borges's
advantage, for some of his earlier critical writing, which would have
been better left in the decent obscurity it enjoys in Spanish, goes on
being dragged into English.) The interest in Borges has one advan-
tage, however, in that his work has been translated by many hands,
giving English readers a choice of versions, and a chance to realize
what every translator must: that there is no such thing as a definitive
translation. Something of the same is true of Neruda's work, and it
has benefited particularly from the variety of its translators, since he
was so many different poets himself; but, however assiduously he is
mined, his work is so vast that only a fraction of it is likely to come
satisfactorily into English. He waits, in his fullness, in Spanish. For
that reason, I am discouraged from continuing to translate Neruda;
but every now and then a poem of his so startles and absorbs me
that its equivalence begins to form in English, and I make a version,
for the awe of it. Translation becomes an addiction in one special
sense: one can always count on it to take one again and again to the
threshold of linguistic astonishment.

It is worth noting that both Neruda and Borges put in time as
translators. Neruda produced an energetic translation of *Romeo and
Juliet* in 1964, and Borges was an early translator of James Joyce, of
Virginia Woolf's *Orlando*, and of William Faulkner, the American
writer who, with Whitman, has had the most pervasive influence
on Latin American writing. As might be expected, translation has
always mesmerized Borges. In an essay on versions of Homer, he
has a sentence that is also destined for my wall. "No problem is as

97

consubstantial with the modest mystery of literature," he writes, "as that posed by a translation."

*

"Anything to do with Latin America never sells" used to be a half-humorous maxim in English publishing circles; but with time the opposite has turned out to be true. There was a point in the mid-sixties when publishers began to take that continent very seriously indeed and became literary prospectors, bent on staking their claims. Such avid attention propelled Latin American writers into a period of prominence that is commonly referred to as *el Boom*, and certainly there seemed more than coincidence to the fact that so many good novelists should be producing such rich work at once, all over the continent. Is there something about the Latin American experience, apart from its labyrinthine variety and the fact that it is largely unwritten as yet, that makes it exceptionally fertile ground for inventive fiction? The clue lies, possibly, in a phrase used by the Cuban novelist Alejo Carpentier in an introduction, written in Haiti, to his own novel *El Reino de Este Mundo*. I quote the relevant passage:

[In Haiti] I was discovering, with every step, the marvellous in the real. But it occurred to me furthermore that the energetic presence of the marvellous in the real was not a privilege peculiar to Haiti, but the heritage of all [Latin] America, which, for example, has not finished fixing the inventory of its cosmogonies. The marvellous in the real is there to find at any moment in the lives of the men who engraved dates on the history of the continent, and left behind names which are still celebrated. . . . The fact is that, in the virginity of its landscape, in its coming together, in its ontology, in the Faustian presence of Indian and Negro, in the sense of revelation arising from its recent discovery, in the fertile mixtures of race which it engendered, [Latin] America is very far from having used up its abundance of mythologies. . . . For what is the story of [Latin] America if not a chronicle of the marvellous in the real?

Lo real maravilloso, the sense of Latin American reality as an amazement, not only physically but also historically, pervades Carpentier's own novels; and it is an element, an aura, that appears in the work of many Latin American writers, however else they may differ in preoccupation and vantage point. The compass of Latin American novels is less that of a total society than of its smaller, more eccentric microcosms—families, villages, tribes, cities, regions. For Latin

98

Americans, theory is the enemy, human eccentricity the norm. *Lo real maravilloso* is a touchstone, not a fiction; and what the Latin American writers are doing, confidently and inventively, is giving it widely varying individual substance, finding for it the language it demands.

The most remarkable incarnation of *lo real maravilloso* to date— and by now almost the definition of it—is the long novel *Cien Años de Soledad*, or *One Hundred Years of Solitude*, by the Colombian writer Gabriel García Márquez, which was first published in Buenos Aires in 1967 and is still reverberating—at last count, in twenty-odd translated versions. The novel has had a legendary publishing history. García Márquez began to write it in January of 1965, and, as it was in progress, it began to take shape as a rumor. The Mexican novelist Carlos Fuentes published a tantalizing intimation of the book in a Mexican review after reading the first seventy-five pages, and fragments appeared in two or three literary magazines—extraordinary parts of an unimaginable whole. When Editorial Sudamericana published the book, it sold out in days and ran through edition after edition in a continent where native best-sellers hardly ever arise. The book was immediately moved by reviewers beyond criticism into that dimension of essential literary experience occupied by *Alice in Wonderland* and *Don Quixote*. Invoked as a classic, in a year it *became* a classic, and García Márquez, to his discomfort, a literary monument. If it was not the Latin Americans' *Don Quixote*, people said, it would do to go on with. It was everybody's book, for, however intricate a construct it was on the metaphysical level, it was founded on the stark anecdotal flow of Latin American experience, and everybody who read it discovered a relative or a familiar in it. (García Márquez told me that following the appearance of the German edition he received a letter from a woman in Bavaria threatening legal action on the ground that he had plagiarized her family history.) I saw a copy of the book sticking out of a taxi-driver's glove compartment in Santiago de Chile a few years ago, and he told me he had read it five times; and a group of students I knew in Buenos Aires used to hold an elaborate running quiz on the book, even using it as the basis for a private language, as enthusiasts once did with Joyce's *Ulysses*.

I have already read two or three books, a cluster of essays and reviews, and a profusion of magazine articles on *One Hundred Years of Solitude*; and there must be an uncountable number of theses, both written and to come, unpicking it over and over. It is a difficult book to deal with critically, since it does not yield to categorization or comparison; and there were some bewildered reviews of it, in England and France especially. García Márquez himself, who is the most generous of spirits, declared early on that, having suffered for years as an itinerant newspaperman, he would not deny interviews to his fellows. "I decided that the best way to put an end to the avalanche of useless interviews is to give the greatest number possible, until the whole world gets bored with me and I'm worn out as a subject," he said in one interview; but the world proved tenacious, and printed conversations with him appeared all over the place—some of them whimsical in the extreme, because he doggedly refuses to translate the book into explanation, and is addicted to playing with language and ideas, if not with his interviewers, for he often refers, cryptically and tantalizingly, to the forty-two undiscovered errors in the text.

The criticism that has accrued around *One Hundred Years of Solitude*—and I have read studies on elements as diverse as the biblical references in the text and the topography of the province of Magdalena, in Colombia, in which both the book and García Márquez are rooted—is the best testimony to his inexhaustibility, and is compulsive reading, in that a classic is a book that one cannot know too much about, a book that deepens with each reading.

The Peruvian writer Mario Vargas Llosa published, in 1971, a 667-page vade mecum entitled *García Márquez: Historia de un Deicidio* (García Márquez: The Story of a Godkiller), a biographical and critical study that painstakingly elucidates the writer's background and influences, his four early books and stories, his preoccupations (or *demonios*, as Vargas Llosa calls them), his literary ancestors, and the writing of *One Hundred Years of Solitude*. Vargas Llosa's book is unlikely to be translated into English, and that is a pity, for it is a most absorbing chronicle of a book's coming into being, of a long and complex creative unwinding. His main claim for the novel is worth quoting in full:

One Hundred Years of Solitude is a *total* novel, in the direct line of those dimensionally ambitious creations that compete with reality on an equal footing, confronting it with the image of a qualitatively equivalent vastness, vitality, and complexity. This totality shows itself first in the plural nature of the novel, in its being apparently contradictory things at once: traditional and modern, local and universal, imaginative and realistic. Another expression of its totality is its limitless accessibility, its quality of being within reach, with distinct but abundant rewards for each one, for the intelligent reader and the imbecile, for the serious person who savors the prose, admires the architecture, and unravels the symbols in a work of fiction, and for the impatient reader who is only after crude anecdote. The literary spirit of our time is most commonly hermetic, oppressed, and minority-centered. *One Hundred Years of Solitude* is one of those rare instances, a major contemporary work of literature that everyone can understand and enjoy.

But *One Hundred Years of Solitude* is a total novel above all because it puts into practice the utopian design of every God-supplanter: to bring into being a complete reality, confronting actual reality with an image that is its expression and negation. Not only does this notion of totality, so slippery and complex, but so inseparable from the vocation of novelist, define the greatness of *One Hundred Years of Solitude*; it gives the clue to it. *One Hundred Years of Solitude* qualifies as a total novel both in its subject matter, to the extent that it describes an enclosed world, from its birth to its death, and all the orders that make it up—individual and collective, legendary and historical, day-to-day and mythical—and in its form, inasmuch as the writing and the structure have, like the material that takes shape in them, an exclusive, unrepeatable, and self-sufficient nature.

One Hundred Years of Solitude, as everyone must know by now, tells the story of the founding of the town of Macondo by José Arcadio Buendía and his wife, Úrsula Iguarán, and of the vagaries of the Buendía family through six generations of plagues, civil war, economic invasion, prosperity, and decline, up to the impending death of the last surviving Buendía and the disintegration of Macondo. The presiding spirit of the Buendía family is the old gypsy magus Melquíades, who, finding the solitude of death unbearable, returns to instruct those members of the family able to see him, and whose coded parchments, deciphered, ultimately, by the last Buendía, prove to be the book we are reading, since Melquíades is able to see backward and forward in time, as the novelist is. Melquíades's parchments "had concentrated a century of daily episodes in such a way that they coexisted in one instant," just as García Márquez has done. Throughout the torrential progress of the book, time is both foreseen and remembered, its natural sequence disrupted by premonition and recurrence. Magical happenings, supernatural perceptions, miracles, and cataclysmic disasters are so closely attendant on characters and events that the book seems to contain all human history compressed into the vicissitudes of a village, and yet each of the Buendías is eccentrically and memorably separate as a character. García Márquez is bewitched by the notion of fiction as a form of magic, which can make free with human time. For the novelist, "everything is known," as Melquíades reiterates in the book. And toward the end of the novel García Márquez observes, in the persona of Aureliano Buendía, that "literature was the best toy ever invented for making fun of people"— a conviction that would certainly be shared by an antic Borges.

The same preoccupation with literature as a secret language is apparent in the fact that García Márquez has strewn the text with personal allusions—dates correspond to the birthdays of his family and friends, his wife appears fleetingly as a character, as he does himself, family jokes are written in—adding to the book a private dimension of his own. In the same way, the book invokes the works of his fellow Latin American novelists. The names of characters from novels of Carlos Fuentes, Julio Cortázar, and Alejo Carpentier crop up in the text, a passage recalls Juan Rulfo, and there are scenes consciously in the manner of Carpentier, Asturias, and Vargas Llosa, in a kind of affectionate homage. "Every good novel is a riddle of the world," García Márquez remarked to Vargas Llosa; and the more one discovers about the book and its genesis—thanks largely to Vargas Llosa—the more one realizes that García Márquez emptied himself into it totally. It is the coming into being of the book, in fact, that turns out to be the most revealing clue to its extraordinary nature.

To Vargas Llosa, García Márquez made a statement that would appear to be another of his whimsies except for the fact that he has emphasized the point many times. "Everything I have written I knew or I had heard before I was eight years old," he said. "From that time on, nothing interesting has happened to me." Talking to the critic Plinio Apuleyo Mendoza, he also said, "In my books, there is not a single line that is not founded on a real happening. My family and my old friends are well aware of it. People say to me, 'Things just happen to you that happen to no one else.' I think they happen to everybody, but people don't have the sensibility to take them in or the disposition to notice them." *One Hundred Years of Solitude* is so full of improbable happenings and apparently grotesque invention that it seems at first perverse of García Márquez to claim these as part of his boyhood experience. Yet I think that these statements have to be taken very seriously indeed, for, on examination, they throw a great deal of light on the genesis and nature of the novel.

*

García Márquez was born in 1928 in the township of Aracataca, in the Colombian province of Magdalena, in the swampy region between the Caribbean and the mountains, and for the first eight years of his life—the crucial years, by his own account—his parents left him behind in Aracataca, in the care of his maternal grandparents, Colonel Nicolás Márquez Iguarán and Doña Tranquilina Iguarán Cotes. His grandparents had settled in Aracataca when it was little more than a village, in the wake of the pulverizing civil war, the War of a Thousand Days, which lasted from 1899 until 1903, and in which Colonel Márquez had fought on the Liberal side against the Conservatives, Aracataca itself being a Liberal outpost. They had lived there through the frenzied years of the "green gold"—the banana fever that brought foreign exploiters and relative prosperity to the region and then subsided around 1920 in a wave of disaffection and economic distress. The grandparents were first cousins, and enjoyed a position of esteem in Aracataca, occupying the most prominent house in the place—a house that they peopled with stories. It was through his grandparents that the bulk of the material that later gushed out in *One Hundred Years of Solitude* entered García Márquez's awareness; they remain, he says, the dominant influence in his life, in their separate ways. Vargas Llosa's account of the novelist's childhood draws attention to circumstances and events in these early years that later found their place in the novel. One of García Márquez's earliest memories is of his grandfather's leading him by the hand through the town to see a traveling circus—a foreshadowing of the first chapter of the novel. The Colonel would read to the boy from the encyclopedia and from *The Thousand and One Nights*, the only books he remembers from these years, and would ply him with stories of the civil war, in which the Colonel had been a companion-in-arms of the Liberal General Rafael Uribe Uribe, whose exploits became the model for Colonel Aureliano Buendía in the novel. To read the history of the War of a Thousand Days is bizarre enough; but to have it recounted and embellished by an old man who took part in it, and who must in any case have assumed mythic proportions for the boy, must have lodged all that material deep enough for it to go undented by fact or subsequent experience. Tales of the banana fever, which brought Aracataca a sudden prosperity and a foreign population, reached him in the same way—from the people who had lived through it. His grandfather waited throughout his life for a chimerical pension promised to Liberal veterans by the Conservatives but never delivered—a state of affairs that is the spine of García Márquez's earlier and most celebrated story, "No One Writes to the Colonel," a noble invocation of the spirit of his grandfather. There are other precise precedents: as a young man, Colonel Márquez had been forced to kill a man in a dispute and, although in the right, had had to settle in a new town—the same circumstance that leads to the founding of Macondo by José Arcadio Buendía. García Márquez remembers his grandfather's saying to him repeatedly, "You cannot imagine how much a dead man weighs." Colonel Márquez also fathered a crop of illegitimate sons during the civil wars, as does Colonel Aureliano Buendía in the novel. Already, the two worlds are difficult to keep separate. People, events past and present, real and fabulous, the encyclopedia and *The Thousand and One Nights*—all occupy the same dimension.

García Márquez has always claimed that his literary style came from his grandmother, Doña Tranquilina; and she is certainly the source of the novel's extraordinary women, whose domestic intuitions challenge the excessive and often misguided rationality of the men. He recalls her waking him up in bed to tell him stories; and she would keep up a running conversation in the large, empty house with dead relatives, so that to him the house seemed peopled with presences. She appears to have drawn no distinction between legend and event, nor would any such distinction have made much sense to García Márquez at that time. It is to her that he attributes the blurring of the magical with the real. In an interview with Plinio Apuleyo Mendoza, he cites one example:

When I was about five, an electrician came to our house to change the meter. He came a number of times. On one of them, I found my grandmother trying to shoo a yellow butterfly from the kitchen with a cloth and muttering, "Every time that man comes, this yellow butterfly appears in the house."

The memory is transmogrified in the novel into the character of Mauricio Babilonia, whose appearances are always accompanied by yellow butterflies. Another of the magical happenings in the novel—when Remedios the Beauty, an unearthly creature beyond human love, whose appearance drives men wild, ascends one day into Heaven as she is folding sheets in the garden—is clarified by García Márquez in conversation with Vargas Llosa:

> The explanation of that is much simpler, much more banal than it appears. There was a girl who corresponded exactly to my description of Remedios in the book. Actually, she ran away from home with a man, and the family, not wishing to face the shame of it, announced, straight-faced, that they had seen her folding sheets in the garden and that afterward she had ascended into Heaven. At the moment of writing, I preferred the family's version to the real one.

Similarly, the strike of banana workers in the novel, which ends in their being massacred, is based on the killing of striking banana workers in Ciénaga, in the province of Magdalena, in 1928. García Márquez remembers hearing stories of it as a boy, but at the same time hearing it denied by others, who accepted the official lie, that it had never happened, just as the survivors in Macondo are made to disremember it. As a boy, listening to the running fables of Aracataca, he drew no line between the fabulous and the real, the true and the false, the subjective and the objective. With the stories, a world entered whole into his imagination. The problem when he faced the writing of *One Hundred Years of Solitude* was to find a way of reproducing that wholeness.

Without further example, I think we can take García Márquez with complete seriousness when he talks of the superimportance of those first eight years. They also throw light on the "solitude" of the title, which is the solitude he describes himself as experiencing in the vast house in Aracataca, with its ghosts and its stories, temporarily abandoned by his own parents to the care of the two eccentric grandparents, whose lives seemed so remote from his own. All the Buendías in the book are similarly enclosed in the glass bubbles of their own destinies, fulfilling separate fates, touching one another only briefly, in passing, possessed by their own secrets.

Given that his early life was a tangible experiencing of *lo real maravilloso*, this was far from a guarantee that García Márquez was to become a writer; if that were so, we should be knee-deep in extraordinary novels. More had to happen; and perhaps the decisive experience was a journey García Márquez took with his mother back to Aracataca to sell the house of his grandparents some seven years after he had left it, on their death. He describes the shock of discovering the town, and the house of his childhood, transposed by time, shrunken, empty, altered. The experience, he says, imprinted deeply in him the desire to find and preserve the Aracataca of his grandparents, the wholeness of his first world; he could not credit that it no longer existed. It did exist; or, at least, it would. On that same journey, Aracataca was metamorphosed into Macondo, the mythical Aracataca of his boyhood; for as the train came to a halt close to the town he saw out of its window the name Macondo on a sign. Macondo was the name of a run-down banana plantation; but it also had a certain currency in local legend as a kind of never-never land from which people did not return.

From that point on, García Márquez lived an itinerant life that produced four books, stories, film scripts, and a slew of newspaper articles. He began, very young, a book—which he never finished—called *La Casa*, an evocation of the legendary house of his grandparents. He threw himself into a literary apprenticeship, reading Amadís de Gaul, Defoe, Rabelais, Balzac, Hemingway, Faulkner, Virginia Woolf, Camus—all the authors who have been invoked as influences on his work. But he was after something in which they could only assist him. He became a journalist, first in Colombia, then in Europe and the United States, turning his attention to writing on his own when he could; but these were turbulent years for him, and the book inside him seemed perpetually out of reach. It was not until he was settled in Mexico in the sixties, writing film scripts after a period of barrenness, that he suddenly found what he had been seeking so long—the focus and the manner ample enough to contain the wholeness of his early vision. He describes to Vargas Llosa how, one day in January of 1965, he was driving his family from Mexico City to Acapulco when the book tugged imperatively at his sleeve. "It was so clear that I could have dictated the first chapter there and then, word for word." He turned the car, went back to Mexico City, closeted himself for the next eighteen months, working every day without letup, and emerged at the end with the complete manuscript of *One Hundred Years of Solitude*, which was immediately accepted by Editorial Sudamericana, in Buenos Aires, and was published, in June of 1967, with almost no emendations.

The four books García Márquez wrote on the way to *One Hun-*

dred Years of Solitude—the novel *La Hojarasca* (*Leaf Storm*), pub-
lished in 1955; the long story "El Coronel No Tiene Quien Le Es-
criba" ("No One Writes to the Colonel"), published in 1958; the
novel *La Mala Hora* (*The Evil Hour*), of 1961; and the collection
of stories *Los Funerales de la Mamá Grande* (*Big Mama's Funeral*),
of 1962—are now, inevitably, combed by readers for any signs of
and references to the huge flowering that followed; and, indeed, *Leaf
Storm* is set in Macondo, which also makes a more substantial ap-
pearance in *Big Mama's Funeral*. It is easy to understand the frustra-
tion García Márquez felt on the publication of each book, for he had
not yet found a way of writing adequate to contain and keep whole
the intricate vision he had of his own many-layered Macondo. But
the early books show him to be a considerable story writer; "No One
Writes to the Colonel" is a meticulously well-written, spare story, its
character beautifully drawn. The early stories are understated and
ironic, but by the time García Márquez came to write the story "Big
Mama's Funeral" the surface realism had begun to crack, and excur-
sions of fancy intruded into the narrative. In the novels, too, he was
experimenting—in *Leaf Storm* with writing of the same reality from
different vantage points, and in *The Evil Hour* with the complexi-
ties of a text within a text. But a spare realism could not contain
the bulging of the imagination that was showing up increasingly in
his work.

Two things were still lacking to the novelist—a unifying tone and
manner to contain the immense running narrative, and some device
to allow him the all-seeing vantage point he required as narrator. It
is worth taking another look at where García Márquez stood in re-
lation to the material, the unwritten book, at this stage. He had clear
and detailed in his head the magical Macondo narrated to him whole
by his grandparents, and the boy's perception of it in its wholeness,
and he had the memory of going back later and perceiving its disin-
tegration, its death. This double perception made him into a magical
being, a child with foreknowledge. The novelist also has foreknowl-
edge. But what must have eluded García Márquez all this time was
where and how to situate himself in relation to his narrative.

The solution, clearly, must have come to him in the form of Mel-
quíades, the old gypsy magus, who is befriended by José Arcadio
Buendía, the founder of Macondo, and who occasionally returns
from death to attend certain of the Buendías. Melquíades knows past

and future. He records the whole history of the Buendía family in code on his parchments, but they are condemned to live in time, and cannot know it. So as Melquíades the novelist could situate himself in the proper magical relation to his narrative, since for him, too, everything is known. Melquíades's parchments are to be the novel.

The first sentence of the novel shows just what use García Márquez makes of his magical persona: "Many years later, as he faced the firing squad, Colonel Aureliano Buendía was to remember that distant afternoon when his father took him to discover ice." In it we are projected forward from the present to a vantage point in the future from which we look backward at what is taking place. We are situated in both dimensions at once. Thus the story is told, looking backward, of a present full of premonition; and memory and dream and fable and miracle are able to intrude into the narrative without any inconsistency. The novel as story is freed from linear time, and sentences are able to refer backward and forward, although firmly rooted in the physicality of the present. "When the pirate Sir Francis Drake attacked Riohacha in the sixteenth century, Úrsula Iguarán's great-great-grandmother became so frightened with the ringing of alarm bells and the firing of cannons that she lost control of her nerves and sat down on a lighted stove." The accident causes her family to move to a settlement where they befriend the Buendía family, and is repeatedly invoked as the initiatory event in the eventual history of Macondo, for Úrsula eventually marries José Arcadio Buendía and, as a consequence, "every time that Úrsula became exercised over her husband's mad ideas, she would leap back over three hundred years of fate and curse the day that Sir Francis Drake had attacked Riohacha." The remote past crops up in the running present; the generations of the Buendías reflect one another, forward and backward. And as Aureliana Babilonia, the last surviving Buendía, is given by his imminent death the insight to decode the parchments of Melquíades, he discovers "that Sir Francis Drake had attacked Riohacha only so that they could seek each other through the most intricate labyrinths of blood until they would engender the mythological animal that was to bring the line to an end." The narrative continues: "It was foreseen that the city of mirrors (or mirages) would be wiped out by the wind and exiled from the memory of men at the precise moment when Aureliano Babilonia would finish deciphering the parchments, and that everything written on them was unrepeatable since time immemorial and forever more, because races condemned to one hundred years of solitude did not have a second opportunity on earth."

*

In a long published interview with Fernández Brasó, García Márquez spoke of his search for a style:

I had to live twenty years and write four books of apprenticeship to discover that the solution lay at the very root of the problem: I had to tell the story, simply, as my grandparents told it, in an imperturbable tone, with a serenity in the face of evidence which did not change even though the world were falling in on them, and without doubting at any moment what I was telling, even the most frivolous or the most truculent, as though these old people had realized that in literature there is nothing more convincing than conviction itself.

It is the word "imperturbable" that leaps out; it is the key to the running tone of *One Hundred Years of Solitude*. Surprising events are chronicled without any expression of surprise, and comic events with a straight face; the real and the magical are juxtaposed without comment or judgment; the dead and living interact in the same unaltering prose dimension. García Márquez is an accomplished exaggerator, as was his grandfather, by repute; but his Neruda-like lists of wonders have a numerical exactness which humanizes them and makes them into facts of perception. The rains that devastate Macondo last "for four years, eleven months, and two days." The astonishing is made matter-of-fact, and the matter-of-fact is a running astonishment: "Colonel Aureliano Buendía organized thirty-two armed uprisings and he lost them all. He had seventeen male children by seventeen different women and they were exterminated one after the other on a single night before the oldest one had reached the age of thirty-five. He survived fourteen attempts on his life, seventy-three ambushes, and a firing squad." The spinster Amaranta Buendía has a clear and unperturbed premonition of her own death:

She saw it because it was a woman dressed in blue with long hair, with a sort of antiquated look, and with a certain resemblance to Pilar Ternera during the time when she had helped with the chores in the kitchen. . . . Death did not tell her when she was going to die . . . but ordered her to begin sewing her own shroud on the next sixth of April. She was authorized to make it as complicated and as fine as she wanted . . . and she was told that she would die without pain, fear, or bitterness at dusk on the day that she finished it. Trying to waste the most time possible, Amaranta ordered some rough flax and spun the thread herself. She did it so carefully that the work alone took four years. Then she started the sewing. . . . One week before she calculated that she would take the last stitch on the night of February 4, and, without revealing the motives, she suggested to Meme that she move up a clavichord concert that she had arranged for the day after. . . . At eight in the morning, she took the last stitch in the most beautiful piece of work that any woman had ever finished, and she announced without the least bit of dramatics that she was going to die at dusk. She not only told the family but the whole town, because Amaranta had conceived of the idea that she could make up for a life of meanness with one last favor to the world, and she thought that no one was in a better position to take letters to the dead.

The book is rooted in the domestic detail of the Buendía household; tragedy, disaster, and death are accommodated, along with magical events, as they intrude into the continuing life of the family. One of the Buendía sons is shot in another part of Macondo:

A trickle of blood came out under the door, crossed the living room, went out into the street, continued on in a straight line across the uneven terraces, went down steps and climbed over curbs, passed along the Street of the Turks, turned a corner to the right and another to the left, made a right angle at the Buendía house, went in under the closed door, crossed through the parlor, hugging the walls so as not to stain the rugs, went on to the other living room, made a wide curve to avoid the dining-room table, went along the porch with the begonias, and passed without being seen under Amaranta's chair as she gave an arithmetic lesson to Aureliano José, and went through the pantry and came out in the kitchen, where Úrsula was getting ready to crack thirty-six eggs to make bread.

In addition to maintaining its even, unsurprised tone, the narrative is reduced starkly to its physical essentials; the astonishment is left to the reader. The novel is crowded with events and characters, comic, grotesque, real and unreal (the distinction no longer has meaning), and the transitions are bland and direct. The touchstone is the running narrative of the writer's grandparents, as perceived by the innocent, unjudging, undifferentiating eye of the boy in Aracataca. When movies are first shown in Macondo, the townspeople "became indignant over the living images that the prosperous merchant Bruno Crespi projected in the theatre with the lion-head ticket windows, for a character who had died and was buried in one film and for whose misfortune tears of affliction had been shed would reappear alive and transformed into an Arab in the next one," and "the audience, who paid two cents apiece to share the difficulties of the actors, would not tolerate that outlandish fraud and they broke up the seats." In Macondo, the wheel is invented with daily regularity.

But the ruthless paring down to physical essentials and the even, matter-of-fact tone are not the only distinguishing features of the book's style; its other remarkable element is its rhythm, its flow. The sentences are constructed with a running inevitability to them. The narrative never pauses but flows on, impervious to the events, disastrous and wondrous, it relates; it is time flowing, the steady current of day-to-day detail. In that flow everything is synthesized and swept along, everything is contained. It is the rhythm that lends the book its feeling of process. Nothing stops the flow of the narrative. Conversations are gnomic exchanges in passing. The book flows on like running water to its inevitable end, which leave us holding the deciphered version of Melquíades's parchments, ready to begin them again.

Things go round again in the same cycles; progress is an illusion, change merely an attribute of time—these attitudes implicit in the book exude from the history and being not just of Aracataca\Macondo and Colombia but of the Latin American continent. Yet the manner in which this fate is accepted and come to terms with is what gives Latin Americans their distinguishing humanity; their measure is a human one. The solitude of the Buendías is their fate; but their reactions to that fate are supremely human—obsessively Promethean and absurdly courageous on the part of the men, tenacious and down-to-earth on the part of the women—and are always leavened with a humorous energy. They assume to the full the responsibility of being their idiosyncratic selves. For the inhabitants of Macondo, there is no body of outside knowledge to refer to. What they know is what they perceive; what they come to terms with is their fate, their own death. García Márquez's twin obsessions— with the original, eccentric sense of human awe lodged in him as a child, and with the discovery of a language ample enough to contain that view in its wholeness—come together so inextricably in *One Hundred Years of Solitude* that the world becomes a book.

The degree to which *One Hundred Years of Solitude* has been acclaimed in translation is a measure of how successful García Márquez is in universalizing his material. Almost monotonously, the book has been named best foreign novel as it has emerged in other languages.

The Italians and the Yugoslavs turned apoplectic in their praise of it, while English reviewers almost universally referred to it as "a fantasy"—a term one must be extremely cautious about applying to García Márquez. Obviously, the book was not being lost in translation; but then for a translator it raises no insurmountable technical problems. The language is crystal-clear and physical, the wordplay is minimal, the vocabulary exotic but containable. The challenge for a translator lies in reproducing the extraordinary running rhythm of the original—García Márquez's sentences are carefully phrased, musically, for the ear; the narrative movement is orchestrated by their rhythm, as García Márquez's own recorded reading of the first chapter makes particularly clear. I can only wonder whether the rhythm of the original is possible to maintain in languages with a sound pattern drastically different from Spanish. But where the rhythm is concerned the English translation, by Gregory Rabassa, is something of a masterpiece, for it is almost matched to the tune of the Spanish, never lengthening or shortening sentences but following them measure for measure. García Márquez insists that he prefers the English translation to the original, which is tantamount to saying they are interchangeable—the near-unattainable point of arrival for any translator.

*

The enthusiastic attention universally attracted by *One Hundred Years of Solitude* propelled García Márquez into a limelight he had not reckoned on, and for a time he became the running prey of literary interviewers and inquisitors, and the center of international curiosity. The question that preoccupied readers most—as it must have preoccupied him—was, What could he write next? *One Hundred Years of Solitude* had freed him from the obsessive preoccupation with unloading into language the Aracataca of his grandparents as he had perceived it; yet it had put a strain of expectation on his work. In 1972, he published a collection of seven new stories, under the title *La Increíble y Triste Historia de la Cándida Eréndira y de su Abuela Desalmada* (*The Incredible and Sad Tale of Innocent Eréndira and Her Heartless Grandmother*). The title story had had two previous existences—one as a long anecdote in *One Hundred Years of Solitude*, and the other as a film script—and now it arrived in a longer and more exotic version, like a written circus. Eréndira burns down her grandmother's house by accident, and she, in revenge, prostitutes her granddaughter in carnival procession through the villages of an interminable desert landscape to recoup her losses. The bare bones of the anecdote are fleshed out in the story, however, with an exuberance of detail and a mythic extension that clearly carry over from the novel; and in the other stories the realistic surface of things has all but disappeared. "The Sea of Lost Time," "A Very Old Man with Enormous Wings," "The Handsomest Drowned Man in the World," "Blacamán the Good, Vendor of Miracles," "The Last Voyage of the Ghost Ship": the titles alone give some indication of where we are—face to face with magical events and extraordinary figures that, although they are no longer in Macondo, belong to the same dimension and wavelength, in which wonders are natural happenings. Most conspicuously, the style continues in the vein of exotic enumeration, imperturbably precise in the face of wonders.

One of the stories, "The Last Voyage of the Ghost Ship," is written in a manner that attempts to bring all its elements into a fusion even tighter than in the novel. Once a year a boy in a seaside village has the vision of a huge liner without lights sailing across the bay in front of the village. He is disbelieved, first by his mother and then, on a subsequent occasion, by the villagers, who beat and ridicule him, so the following year he lies in wait, in a stolen rowboat, and leads the liner aground on the shoal in front of the village church. The story, dense in physical detail, is a running narrative of six pages, a single sentence that encompasses past and dream as part of a flowing present, a stream of consciousness not confined to any one consciousness—for characters intrude in the first person, the focal point keeps shifting, the objective and the subjective are parts of a larger whole. Again, the images are threaded on the continuing string of the rhythm. It was clear from this story that García Márquez had not yet satisfied his linguistic curiosity.

Extravagant of imagination, these stories showed him more determined than ever to embrace the wondrous as part of the natural— to destroy the distinction, to insist on the marvellous as real. He also seemed to be trying to embed linear narrative episodically in a larger language; but he could not abandon it, for he is an instinctive storyteller, most probably because of his profound experience as a listener. The compulsion intrudes into his conversation; he enfables his day. On one occasion, in Barcelona, when we met after an interim, I noticed that he had given up smoking—surprisingly, for he had been a fierce smoker. "I will tell you how to be free of smoking," he said to me. "First, you must decide that the cigarette, a dear friend who has been close to you for many years, is about to die. Death, as we know, is irremediable. You take a pristine packet of your favorite cigarettes—mine were those short black Celtas—and you bury it, with proper ceremony, in a grave you have prepared in the garden—I made a headstone for mine. Then, every Sunday—not oftener, for the memory is painful—you put flowers on the grave, and give thanks. Time passes. For me now, the cigarette is dead, and I have given up mourning."

In occasional interviews, García Márquez spoke of the book he was writing: a phantasmagorical study of a dictator who has lived for two hundred years; an exploration of the solitude of power. The book was a long time in the writing, and was promised long before it arrived, but was eventually published in March of 1975 under the title of *El Otoño del Patriarca*. The first Spanish reviews were tinged with disappointment, since the reviewers obviously wanted to be back in Macondo. It took time for the book to separate itself from the powerful shadow of *One Hundred Years of Solitude*. Besides, it is a book requiring very attentive reading at first, until one grows more comfortably familiar with its extraordinary style, for it goes even further, along the lines of "The Last Voyage of the Ghost Ship," toward fusing all its sprawling elements into one single stream of prose.

The book is set in an unspecified Caribbean country which is under the sway of a dictator who has lived longer than anyone can remember; and it is no more specific of time and place than that. Its point of departure—and the starting point for each of its six chapters—is a mob breaking into the decaying palace to find the dictator dead. As they poke wonderingly among the ruins of the palace, with "the felt on the billiard tables cropped by cows," they begin to brood, in their collective consciousness, on incidents in the dictator's reign, and the narrative shifts to these events, then passes without pausing into the dictator's consciousness, back into events and other consciousnesses, in continuous change. Linear time is abandoned, and even deliberately confused; everyone has forgotten the sequence of events while vividly remembering and juxtaposing the events themselves. Each chapter encompasses two or three crucial episodes in the

dictator's career—set pieces of the imagination, like separate García
Márquez stories inserted in the flow—alongside the natural and un-
natural disasters: the occasional massacres of plotting generals, the
coming of a comet, the occupation of the country by marines of a
foreign power, the eventual selling of the country's sea. The dictator
himself is never named, and there are only a few fully rounded, fully
identified characters: the dictator's mother, Benedición Alvarado,
the simple woman who accompanies him anxiously into power, and
in whose memory, when his attempts to canonize her have failed,
he declares war against the Holy See; his crony General Rodrigo de
Aguilar, who, when he is discovered to be a traitor, is served up by
the dictator, roasted and garnished, at a feast of his brother officers;
the novice nun Leticia Nazareno, whom he impulsively marries and
is dominated by, and who, with her young son, already a general,
is torn to pieces by specially trained wild dogs; Manuela Sánchez,
the gypsy queen, who beguiles the dictator into transforming sub-
urbs for her pleasure; José Ignacio Saenz de la Barra, his sleek and
sinister favorite, who initiates a reign of terror the dictator can only
survive, not control. The narrative keeps being picked up by other
voices, other consciousnesses, always sharp in physical detail. There
is a pervading domesticity to García Márquez's frame of reference;
in one long passage we follow the dictator through the long and
finicky ritual of going to bed, in the course of which he patrols the
palace, dressing objects in asides of memory.

Technically, what García Márquez does in *The Autumn of the
Patriarch* is to dispense with the sentence altogether as the unit of
his prose, and substitute an intelligible flow that encompasses several
shifts in vantage point. In one passage, the dictator is being besieged
in his palace:

I already told you not to pay them any heed, he said, dragging his graveyard
feet along the corridors of ashes and scraps of carpets and singed tapestries,
but they're going to keep it up, they told him, they had sent word that the
flaming balls were just a warning, that the explosions will come after general
sir, but he crossed the garden without paying attention to anyone, in the last
shadows he breathed in the sound of the newborn roses, the disorders of the
cocks in the sea wind, what shall we do general, I already told you not to pay
any attention to them, God damn it, and as on every day at that hour he went
to oversee the milking, so as on every day at that hour the insurrectionists
in the Conde barracks saw the mule cart with the six barrels of milk from
the presidential stable appear, and in the driver's seat there was the same

lifetime carter with the oral message that the general sends you this milk even though you keep on spitting in the hand that feeds you, he shouted it out with such innocence that General Bonivento Barboza gave the order to accept it on the condition that the carter taste it first so that they could be sure it wasn't poisoned, and then they opened the iron gates and the fifteen hundred rebels looking down from the inside balconies saw the cart drive in to center on the paved courtyard, they saw the orderly climb up onto the driver's seat with a pitcher and a ladle to give the carter the milk to taste, they saw him uncork the first barrel, they saw him floating in the ephemeral backwash of a dazzling explosion and they saw nothing else to the end of time in the volcanic heat of the mournful yellow mortar building in which no flower ever grew, whose ruins remained suspended for an instant in the air from the tremendous explosion of the six barrels of dynamite.

What García Márquez is after is a language that can contain individual consciousnesses but is not confined by any one, a language that can encompass a whole human condition, that can accommodate the contradictory illusions of which it is made up. Objective truth is only one illusion among a number of illusions, individual and tribal. Consciousness can be neither linear nor serial. The text, though still as sharp in physical particulars as ever, raises infinitely more problems for the translator than its predecessor did, for its sudden shifts in focus have to be handled in language in such a way as to take the reader's attention with them. Rabassa manages these beautifully. Again, his version is more than a translation: it is a matching in English of the original.

The book's preoccupation is with appearance, deception, and illusion, with lies transformed into illusions by the power of belief. Behind illusion there is only solitude—in this case, the solitude of power. The dictator, who can neither read nor write, governs "orally and physically." His power is beyond reason:

you find him alive and bring him to me and if you find him dead bring him to me alive and if you don't find him bring him to me, an order so unmistakable and fearsome that before the time was up they came to him with the news general sir that they had found him.

The only person ever to tell him the truth is his double, Patricio Aragonés, as he is dying of poison meant for the dictator, but the dictator knows that truth is only his own whim, and language only another deception. Tuned in to the betrayals of others, he survives long beyond the point where his power has any meaning, a shambling old man-child trying to get a night's rest for his accompanying infirmities from his own grotesque and imperturbable image. Close to death (his second death, since he used the death of his double in order to claim rebirth), he broods:

> he learned to live with those and all the miseries of glory as he discovered in the course of his uncountable years that a lie is more comfortable than doubt, more useful than love, more lasting than truth, he had arrived without surprise at the ignominious fiction of commanding without power, of being exalted without glory and of being obeyed without authority.

The illusion of his power is, however, sustained by everyone around him, so that he has no choice but to wear it. He keeps alive by his acute cunning, his nose for deception; at one point (after he has been taught to read by Leticia Nazareno), "the final oracles that governed his fate were the anonymous graffiti on the walls of the servants' toilets, in which he would decipher the hidden truths that no one would have dared reveal to him, not even you, Leticia, he would read them at dawn on his way back from the milking. . . . broadsides of hidden rancor which matured in the warm impunity of the toilets and ended up coming out onto the streets." Fictions outlive the need for them but refuse to die. The only refuge from deceptions is in solitude, yet it is out of solitude that we create the fictions to sustain us.

In *The Autumn of the Patriarch* García Márquez moves toward a complete mythifying of experience, into a total flow that cannot be checked by any reality. Realities of Colombian history occur as fact, legend, and lie, all three; rumor, gossip, fairy tale, dream, illusion, memory all tumble over one another in the book's perception. It has to be taken whole, for wholeness, again, is what it is after. The grossness of its cruelties and lecheries is told in an even, unwavering tone, grotesque in detail; they are part of the book's condition. García Márquez is more concerned with dictatorship as myth in the popular mind (that fountain of invention to which he appears to have unlimited access). Like *One Hundred Years of Solitude*, the book ought to be given three or four readings, for it deserves them, and rewards them. It is a formidable piece of invention, and it pushes the discoveries of *One Hundred Years of Solitude* further, closer to a contained whole. García Márquez's writing has always been illuminated by the transformations his imagination is capable of making, the humanity of his perception, his accurate astonishment, even on the small scale, in a phrase or a minor incident. Patricio Aragonés upbraids the dictator for "making me drink turpentine so I would forget how to read and write." The dictator, waking up suddenly in fear, "felt that the ship of the universe had reached some port while he was asleep." And, we are told, "on one national holiday she [the dictator's mother] had made her way through the guard of honor with a basket of empty bottles and reached the presidential limousine that was leading the parade of celebration in an uproar of ovations and martial music and storms of flowers and she shoved the basket through the window and shouted to her son that since you'll be passing right by take advantage and return these bottles to the store on the corner, poor mother." The "stigma of solitude" can be made bearable only by the transforming imagination, as it was in the tales told García Márquez by his grandparents, as it is in his own inexhaustible capacity for containing these transformations in language. He abundantly outdoes his origins. What García Márquez is showing us all the time is the humanizing power of the imagination. In all his writing, the imagination is no mere whimsey, nor a Latin American eccentricity: it is a way of dealing with the mysteries of existence, an essential tool for survival, as we say nowadays. The people of Macondo live in a world full of mysteries, without access to any explanation. All they can count on to make these mysteries bearable is the transforming power of their own imaginations, through the anecdotes and fictions they construct to bring the world into some kind of equilibrium, to find some kind of comfort for the separate solitudes it is their fate to inhabit.

For García Márquez, the marvelous, which he equates with the human, contains the real, and can transform it at will. "They should take the hens out of their nests when there's thunder so they don't hatch basilisks," says Benedición Alvarado on her deathbed, and at once we know where we are. García Márquez talked to Vargas Llosa about an aunt who haunted the house of his childhood—the same aunt who sewed her own shroud. "Once, she was embroidering in the passage when a girl arrived with a strange-looking hen's egg, an egg with a protuberance," he said. "I don't know why our house served as a kind of consulting room for all the mysteries of the place. Every time anything out of the ordinary cropped up, which nobody understood, they went to the house and asked, and, in the main, this woman, this aunt, always had an answer. What enchanted me was the naturalness with which she settled these questions. To go back to the girl with the egg, she said, 'Look! Why does this egg have a protuberance?' Then my aunt looked at her and said, 'Ah, because it is a basilisk's egg. Light a bonfire on the patio.' They lit the fire and burned the egg as if it were the most natural thing in the world. I think that naturalness gave me the key to *One Hundred Years of Solitude*, where the most terrifying and extraordinary things are re-counted with the same straight face this aunt wore when she said that a basilisk's egg—I didn't know what it was—should be burned on the patio."

In Memoriam, Amada

J U D A S   R O Q U Í N told me this story, on the veranda of his
mildewed house in Cahuita. Years have passed and I may have altered
some details. I cannot be sure.

In 1933, the young Brazilian poet Baltasar Melo published a book
of poems, *Brasil Encarnado*, which stirred up such an outrage that
Melo, forewarned by powerful friends, chose to flee the country.
The poems were extravagant, unbridled even, in their manner, and
applied a running sexual metaphor to Brazilian life; but it was one
section, "Perversions," in which Melo characterized three prominent
public figures as sexual grotesques, that made his exile inevitable.
Friends hid him until he could board a freighter from Recife, under
cover of darkness and an assumed name, bound for Panama. With the
ample royalties from his book, he was able to buy an *estancia* on the
Caribbean coast of Costa Rica, not far from where Roquín lived.
The two of them met inevitably, though they did not exactly become
friends.

Already vain and arrogant by nature, Melo became insufferable
with success and the additional aura of notorious exile. He used his
fame mainly to entice women with literary pretensions, some of them
the wives of high officials. In Brazil, however, he remained something
of a luminary to the young, and his flight added a certain allure to his
reputation, to such a point that two young Bahian poets who worked
as reporters on the newspaper *Folha da Tarde* took a leave of absence
to interview him in his chosen exile. They traveled to Costa Rica
mostly by bus, taking over a month to reach San José, the capital.
Melo's retreat was a further day's journey, and they had to cover the
last eleven kilometers on foot. Arriving at evening, they announced
themselves to the housekeeper. Melo, already half-drunk, was up-

stairs, entertaining the daughter of a campesino, who countenanced the liaison for the sake of his fields. Melo, unfortunately, chose to be outraged, and shouted, in a voice loud enough for the waiting poets to hear, "Tell those compatriots of mine that Brazil kept my poems and rejected me. Poetic justice demands that they return home and wait there for my next book." For the two frustrated pilgrims, the journey back to Bahia was nothing short of nightmare.

*

The following autumn, a letter arrived in Cahuita for Baltasar Melo from a young Bahian girl, Amada da Bonavista, confessing shyly that her reading of *Brasil Encarnado* had altered her resolve to enter a convent, and asking for the poet's guidance. Flattered, titillated, he answered with a letter full of suggestive warmth. In response to a further letter from her, he made so bold as to ask for her likeness, and received in return the photograph of an irresistible beauty. Over the course of a whole year, their correspondence grew increasingly more erotic until, on impulse, Melo had his agent send her a steamship ticket from Bahia to Panama, where he proposed to meet her. Time passed, trying his patience; and then a letter arrived, addressed in an unfamiliar hand, from an aunt of Amada's. She had contracted meningitis and was in a critical condition. Not long after, the campesino's daughter brought another envelope with a Bahia postmark. It contained the steamship ticket, and a newspaper clipping announcing Amada's death.

We do not know if the two poets relished their intricate revenge, for they remain nameless, forgotten. But although it would be hard nowadays to track down an available copy of *Brasil Encarnado*, Baltasar Melo's name crops up in most standard anthologies of modern Brazilian poetry, represented always by the single celebrated poem, "In Memoriam: Amada," which Brazilian schoolchildren still learn by heart. I translate, inadequately of course, the first few lines:

> Body forever in bloom,
> you are the only one
> who never did decay
> go gray, wrinkle, and die
> as all warm others do.
> My life, as it wears away
> owes all its light to you . . .

When Judas had finished, I of course asked him the inevitable question: Did Baltasar Melo ever find out? Did someone tell him? Roquín got up suddenly from the hammock he was sprawled in, and looked out to the white edge of surf, just visible under the rising moon. "Ask me another time," he said. "I haven't decided yet."

POEMS

I have always been grateful to have come first to poetry, before going on to write prose and to translate, for it is through poetry that one experiences language at its most thrilling, in its miraculous compressions of sound, sense, and shape. Poetry engenders not just a deep love of language, but also an unquenchable curiosity over what it can do. The poems that follow are those from my previous collections that seem to me to deserve a continuing existence.

Poem Without Ends

One cannot take the beginning out of the air
saying 'It is the time: the hour is here.'
The process is continuous as wind,
the bird observed, not rising, but in flight,
unrealized, in motion in the mind.

The end of everything is similar, never
actually happening, but always over.
The agony, the bent head, only tell
that already in the heart the innocent evening
is thick with all the ferment of farewell.

Growing, Flying, Happening

Say the soft bird's name, but do not be surprised
to see it fall
headlong, struck skyless, into its pigeonhole—
columba palumbus and you have it dead,
wedged, neat, unwinged in your head.

That that black-backed tatter-winged thing
straking the harbour water and then plummeting
down, to come up, sleek head-a-cock,
a minted herring shining in its beak,
is a *guillemot*, is neither here nor there
in the amazement of its rising,
wings slicing the stiff salt air.

That of that spindling spear-leaved plant,
wearing the palest purple umbel,
many-headed, blue-tinted, stilt-stalked
at the stream-edge, one should say briefly
angelica, is by-the-way (though grant
the name itself to be beautiful).
Grant too that any name
makes its own music, that *bryony, sally-my-handsome*
burst at their sound into flower,
and that *falcon* and *phalarope* fly off in the ear,
still,
names are for saying at home.

The point is seeing—the grace
beyond recognition, the ways
of the bird rising, unnamed, unknown,
beyond the range of language, beyond its noun.
Eyes open on growing, flying, happening,
and go on opening. Manifold, the world
dawns on unrecognizing, realizing eyes.
Amazement is the thing.
Not love, but the astonishment of loving.

Oddments, Inklings, Omens, Moments

Oddments, as when
you see through skin,
when flowers appear
to be eavesdropping,
or music somewhere
declares your mood;
when sleep fulfils
a feel of dying
or fear makes ghosts
of clothes on a chair.

Inklings, as when
some room rhymes
with a lost time,
or a book reads
like a well-known dream;
when a smell recalls
portraits, funerals,
when a wish happens
or a mirror sees
through distances.

Omens, as when
a shadow from nowhere
falls on a wall,
when a bird seems
to mimic your name,
when a cat eyes you
as though it knew
or, heavy with augury,
a crow caws
cras cras from a tree.

Moments, as when
the air's awareness
makes guesses true,
when a hand's touch

speaks past speech
or when, in poise,
two sympathies
lighten each other,
and love occurs
like song, like weather.

Directions for a Map

Birds' eyes see almost this, a tiny island
odd as a footprint on a painted sea.
But maps set margins. Here, the land is measured,
changed to a flat, explicit world of names.

Crossing the threads of roads to nibbled coastlines,
the rivers run in veins that crack the surface.
Mountains are dark like hair, and here and there
lakes gape like moth holes with the sea showing through.

Between the seaports stutter dotted shiplines,
crossing designs of latitude and language.
The towns are flying names. The sea is titled.
A compass crowns the corner like a seal.

Distance is spelt in alphabets and numbers.
Arrows occur at intervals of inches.
There are no signs for love or trouble, only
dots for a village and a cross for churches.

Here space is free for once from time and weather.
The sea has pause. To plot is possible.
Given detachment and a careful angle,
all destinations are predictable.

And given, too, the confidence of distance,
strangers may take a hundred mural journeys.
For once the paths are permanent, the colors
outlast the seasons and the deaths of friends.

And even though, on any printed landscape,
directions never tell you where to go,
maps are an evening comfort to the traveler—
a pencil line will quickly take him home.

The Waterglass

A church tower crowned the town,
double in air and water,
and over anchored houses
the round bells rolled at noon.
Bubbles rolled to the surface.
The drowning bells swirled down.

The sun burned in the bay.
A lighthouse towered downward,
moored in mirroring fathoms.
The seaweed swayed its tree.
The boat below me floated
upside down on the sky.

An underwater wind
ruffled the red-roofed shallows
where wading stilt-legged children
stood in the clouded sand,
and down from the knee-deep harbour
a ladder led to the drowned.

Gulls fell out of the day.
The thrown net met its image
in the window of the water.
A ripple slurred the sky.
My hand swam up to meet me,
and I met myself in the sea.

Mirrored, I saw my face
in the underworld of the water,
and saw my drowned self sway in
the glass day underneath—
till I spoke to my speaking likeness,
and the moment broke with my breath.

Once at Piertarvit

Once at Piertarvit,
one day in April,
the edge of spring,
with the air a-ripple
and sea like knitting,
as Avril and Ann
and Ian and I
walked in the wind
along the headland,
Ian threw an apple
high over Piertarvit.

Not a great throw,
you would say, if you'd seen it,
but good for Ian.
His body tautened,
his arm let go
like a flesh-and-bone bow,
and the hard brown apple
left over from autumn
flew up and up,
crossing our gaze,
from the cliff at Piertarvit.

Then all at once, horror
glanced off our eyes,
Ann's, mine, Avril's.
As the apple curved
in the stippled sky,
at the top of its arc,
it suddenly struck
the shape of a bird,
a gull that had glided
down from nowhere
above Piertarvit.

We imagined the thud
and the thin ribs breaking,
blood, and the bird
hurtling downwards.
No such thing.
The broad wings wavered
a moment only,
then air sustained them.
The gull glided on
while the apple fell
in the sea at Piertarvit.

Nobody spoke.
Nobody whistled.
In that one moment,
our world had shifted.
The four of us stood
stock-still with awe
till, breaking the spell,
Ian walked away
with a whirl in his head.
The whole sky curdled
over Piertarvit.

I followed slowly,
with Ann and Avril
trailing behind.
We had lost our lightness.
Even today,
old as I am,
I find it hard
to say, without wonder,
"Ian hit a bird
with an apple, in April,
once at Piertarvit."

A Game of Glass

I do not believe this room
with its cat and its chandelier,
its chessboard-tiled floor,
its shutters that open out
on an angel playing a fountain,
and the striped light slivering in
to a room that looks the same
in the mirror over my shoulder,
with a second glass-eyed cat.

My book does not look real.
The room and the mirror seem
to be playing a waiting game.
The cat has made its move,
the fountain has one to play,
and the thousand eyes of the angel
in the chandelier above
gleam beadily, and say
the next move is up to me.

How can I trust my luck?
Whatever way I look,
I cannot tell which is the door,
and I do not know who is who—
the thin man in the mirror
or the watery one in the fountain.
The cat is eyeing my book.
What am I meant to do?
Which side is the mirror on?

For Her Sake

Her world is all aware. She reads
omens in small happenings, the fall of a teaspoon,
flurries of birds, a cat's back arching,
words unspoken, wine spilt.
She will notice moods in handwriting,
be tuned to feelings in a room,
sense ill luck in a house, take heed of ghosts,
hear children cry before the sound has reached her,
stay unperturbed in storms, keep silence
where speech would spoil. Days are her changes,
weather her time.

Whether it be becalmed in cool mornings
of air and water, or thunderstruck through nights
where flesh craves and is answered, in her, love
knows no division, is an incarnation
of all her wonder, as she makes
madness subside, and all thought-splintered things
grow whole again.

Look below. She walks in the garden,
preoccupied with paths, head bent,
beautiful, not at rest, as objects are,
but moving, in the fleck of light and shade.
Her ways are hers, not mine. Pointless to make
my sense of her, or claim her faithfulness.
She is as women are, aware
of her own mystery, in her way faithful
to flowers and days; and from the window's distance,
I watch her, haunted by her otherness.

Well to love true women, whose whims are wise,
whose world is warm, whose home is time,
and well to pleasure them, since, last of all,
they are the truth which men must tell,
and in their pleasure, houses lighten,
gardens grow fruitful, and true tales are told.

Well to move from mind's distance
into their aura, where the air
is shifting, intimate, particular.

And of true women, she, whose eyes illumine
this day I wake in—well to mark
her weather, how her look is candid,
her voice clear-toned, her heart private,
her love both wild and reticent.
Well to praise and please her, well to make
this for her sake.

Calenture

He never lives to tell,
but other men bring back the tale

of how, after days of gazing at the sea
unfolding itself incessantly and greenly—
hillsides of water crested with clouds of foam—
he, heavy with a fading dream of home,
clambers aloft one morning and, looking down,
cries out at seeing a different green—
farms, woods, grasslands, an extending plain,
hazy meadows, a long tree-fledged horizon,
his ship riding deep in rippled grain,
swallows flashing in the halcyon sun,
the road well-known to him, the house, the garden,
figures at the gate—and, foundering in his passion,
he suddenly climbs down and begins to run.
Dazed by his joy, the others watch him drown.

Such calenture, they say,
is not unknown in lovers long at sea

yet such a like fever did she make in me
this green-leaved summer morning, that I,
seeing her confirm a wish made lovingly,
felt gate, trees, grass, birds, garden glimmer over,
a ripple cross her face, the sky quiver,
the cropped lawn sway in waves, the house founder,
the light break into flecks, the path shimmer
till, finding her eyes clear and true at the centre,
I walked toward her on the flowering water.

The Figures on the Frieze

Darkness wears off and, dawning into light,
they find themselves unmagically together.
He sees the stains of morning in her face.
She shivers, distant in his bitter weather.

Diminishing of legend sets him brooding.
Great goddess-figures conjured from his book
blur what he sees with bafflement of wishing.
Sulky, she feels his fierce, accusing look.

Familiar as her own, his body's landscape
seems harsh and dull to her habitual eyes.
Mystery leaves, and, mercilessly flying,
the blind fiends come, emboldened by her cries.

Avoiding simple reach of hand for hand
(which would surrender pride) by noon they stand
withdrawn from touch, reproachfully alone,
small in each other's eyes, tall in their own.

Wild with their misery, they entangle now
in baffling agonies of why and how.
Afternoon glimmers, and they wound anew,
flesh, nerve, bone, gristle in each other's view.

"What have you done to me?" From each proud heart,
new phantoms walk in the deceiving air.
As the light fails, each is consumed apart,
he by his ogre vision, she by her fire.

When night falls, out of a despair of daylight,
they strike the lying attitudes of love,
and through the perturbations of their bodies,
each feels the amazing, murderous legends move.

Quarrels

I can feel a quarrel blowing up in your body,
as old salts can smell storms
which are still fretting under the horizon,
before your eyes have flashed their first alarms.

Whatever the reason, the reason is not the reason.
It's a weather. It's a wellhead about to blaze gas,
flaring up when you suddenly stumble over
an alien presence in your private space.

You face me, eyes slitted like a cat's.
I can feel your nails uncurling.
The tendons in your neck twang with anger.
Your face is liquid as it is in loving.

Marking how often you say "always" and "never,"
I on my side grow icy, tall, and thin
until, with watching you, I forget to listen,
and am burned through and through with your high passion.

Face to face, like wrestlers or lovers,
we spit it out. Your words nip, like bites.
Your argument's a small, tenacious creature
I try to stomp on with great logical boots.

Dear angry one, let the boots and the skittering beast
chase wildly round the room like Tom and Jerry
or who and why. Let us withdraw and watch them,
but side by side, not nose to nose and wary.

That is the only way we'll disentangle
the quarrel from ourselves and switch it off.
Not face to face. The sparks of confrontation
too easily ignite a rage like love.

The he-with-her subsides, the I-with-you
looms into place. So we fold up the words
and, with a movement much like waking up,
we turn the weather down, and turn towards.

In Such a Poise Is Love

Why should a hint of winter
shadow the window while the insects enter,
or a feel of snowfall, taking corners off
the rough wall and the roof,
while the sun, hanging in the sky,
hotly denies its contrary?

As if it knew all future must entail
probable tempered by improbable,
so the mind wanders to the unforeseen,
and the eye, waking, poises between
shock and recognition—the clothes, the chair,
bewildering, familiar.

In such a poise is love. But who
can keep the balance true,
can stay in the day's surprise, moving
between twin fears, of losing and of having?
Who has not, in love's fever,
insisted on the fatal vow, "for ever,"
and sensed, before the words are gone,
the doom in them dawn?

Me to You

Summer's gone brown and, with it,
our wanderings in the shires, our ways.
Look at us now.
A shuttered house drips in Moroccan rain.
A mill sits ghostly in the green of France.

Beaches are empty now of all but pebbles.
But still, at crossroads, in senorial gardens,
we meet, sleep, wrangle, part, meet, part,
making a lodging of the heart.

Now that the sea begins to dull with winter,
and I so far, and you so far
(and home further than either),
write me a long letter,
as if from home.
         Tell me about the snowfalls
at night, and tell me how we'd sit in firelight,
hearing dogs huff in sleep, hearing the geese
hiss in the barn, hearing the horse clop home.
Say how the waterfall sounds, and how the weeds
trail in the slithering river.
Write me about the weather.

Perhaps
a letter across water,
something like this, but better,
would almost move us strangely
closer to home.

Write, and I'll come.

II

All day I have been writing you a letter.

Now, after hours of gazing at the page
and watching the screen of rain, I have enacted

a flow of endless letters in my head
(all of them different) and not one
in any written shape to send.
Those letters never end.

In between pages of wishing, I walked to the river
and wrote you of how the water
wrinkles and eddies and wanders away.
That was easier to say.

I wrote of how the snow
had fallen and turned blue,
and how the bush you wanted
could not be planted.

Some pages were all remembering—the places,
faces, frontiers, rooms, and days we went through
ages ago.
(Do you do this too?)
Always coming back to snow.

Mostly an endless, useless run of questions.
How are you now? How is it there?
Who will you and I
be in a year?
Who are we now?

Oh no,
there is no letter to send you, only this stream
of disconnected brooding, this rhythm
of wanting, cumbersome
in words, lame.

Come.

Mediterranean

However gracefully
the spare leaves of the fig tree
abundant overhead
with native courtesy
include us in their shade,
among the rented flowers
we keep a tenant's station.
The garden is not ours.

Under the arching trellis
the gardener moves below.
Observe him on his knees
with offering of water
for roots that are not his
tendering to a power
whose name he does not know,
but whom he must appease.

So do we too accord
the windings of the vine
and swelling of the olive
a serious mute oblation
and a respectful word,
aware of having put,
in spite of cultivation,
the worm within the fruit.

This garden tenancy
tests our habitual eye.
Now, water and the moon
join what we do not own.
The rent is paid in breath,
and so we freely give
the apple tree beneath
our unpossessive love.

Dear one, this present Eden
lays down its own condition:
we should not ask to wait.
No angel drives us out,
but time, without a word,
will show among the flowers,
sure as a flaming sword.
The garden is not ours.

Tiree

Over the walking foreshore cluttered
black with the tide's untidy wrack,
and pools that brimmed with the moon,
I trespassed underwater.
My feet found seabed sand.
The night wore guilt like a watermark
and down the guilty dark,
the gulls muttered to windward.
Far out, the tide spoke back.

Across the morning clean of my walking
ghost and the driftwood litter,
singly I walked into singing light.
The rocks walked light on the water,
and clouds as clean as spinnakers
puffed in the sea-blue sky.
A starfish signed the sand. Beyond,
I faced the innocent sea.

Curiosity

may have killed the cat. More likely,
the cat was just unlucky, or else curious
to see what death was like, having no cause
to go on licking paws, or fathering
litter on litter of kittens, predictably.

Nevertheless, to be curious
is dangerous enough. To distrust
what is always said, what seems,
to ask odd questions, interfere in dreams,
smell rats, leave home, have hunches,
does not endear cats to those doggy circles
where well-smelt baskets, suitable wives, good lunches
are the order of things, and where prevails
much wagging of incurious heads and tails.

Face it. Curiosity
will not cause us to die—
only lack of it will.
Never to want to see
the other side of the hill
or that improbable country
where living is an idyll
(although a probable hell)
would kill us all.
Only the curious
have if they live a tale
worth telling at all.

Dogs say cats love too much, are irresponsible,
are dangerous, marry too many wives,
desert their children, chill all dinner tables
with tales of their nine lives.
Well, they are lucky. Let them be
nine-lived and contradictory,
curious enough to change, prepared to pay
the cat-price, which is to die

and die again and again,
each time with no less pain.
A cat-minority of one
is all that can be counted on
to tell the truth; and what cats have to tell
on each return from hell
is this: that dying is what the living do,
that dying is what the loving do,
and that dead dogs are those who never know
that dying is what, to live, each has to do.

Propinquity

is the province of cats. Living by accident,
lapping the food at hand or sleeking down
in an adjacent lap when sleep occurs to them,
never aspiring to consistency
in homes or partners, unaware of property,
cats take their chances, love by need or nearness
as long as the need lasts, as long as the nearness
is near enough. The code of cats is simply
to take what comes. And those poor souls who claim
to own a cat, who long to recognize
in bland and narrowing eyes a look like love,
are bound to suffer should they expect
cats to come purring punctually home.
Home is only where the food and the fire are,
but might be anywhere. Cats fall on their feet,
nurse their own wounds, attend to their own laundry,
and purr at appropriate times. O folly, folly,
to love a cat, and yet
we dress with love the distance that they keep,
the hair-raising way they have, and easily blame
all their abandoned litters and torn ears
on some marauding tiger, well aware
that cats themselves do not care.

Yet part of us is cat. Confess—
love turns on accident and needs
nearness; and the various selves we have
accrue from our cat-wanderings, our chance
crossings. Imagination prowls at night,
cat-like, among odd possibilities.
Only our dog-sense brings us faithfully home,
makes meaning out of accident, keeps faith,
and, cat-and-dog, the arguments go at it.
But every night, outside, cat-voices call
us out to take a chance, to leave
the safety of our baskets and to let

what happens happen. "Live, live!" they catcall.
"Each moment is your next! Propinquity,
propinquity is all!"

Cat-Faith

As a cat, caught by the door opening,
on the perilous top shelf, red-jawed and raspberry-clawed,
lets itself fall floorward without looking,
sure by cat-instinct it will find the ground,
where innocence is; and falls
anyhow, in a furball, so fast that the eye
misses the twist and trust
that come from having fallen before,
and only notices cat silking away,
crime inconceivable in so meek a walk:

so do we let ourselves fall morningward
through shelves of dream. When, libertine at dark,
we let the visions in, and the black window
grotesques us back, our world unbalances.
Many-faced monsters of our own devising
jostle on the verge of sleep, as the room
loses its edges and grows hazed and haunted
by words murmured or by woes remembered,
till, sleep-dissolved, we fall, the known world leaves us,
and room and dream and self and safety melt
into a final madness, where any landscape
may easily curdle, and the dead cry out . . .

but ultimately, it ebbs. Voices recede.
The pale square of the window glows and stays.
Slowly the room arrives and dawns, and we
arrive in our selves. Last night, last week, the past
leak back, awake. As light solidifies,
dream dims. Outside, the washed hush of the garden
waits patiently and, newcomers from death,
how gratefully we draw its breath!
Yet, to endure that unknown night by night,
must we not be sure, with cat-insight,
we can afford its terrors, and that full day
will find us at the desk, sane, unafraid—
cheeks shaven, letters written, bills paid?

Pigeons

On the crooked arm of Columbus, on his cloak,
they mimic his blind and statuary stare,
and the chipped profiles of his handmaidens
they adorn with droppings. Over the loud square,
from all the arms and ledges of their rest,
only a breadcrust or a bell unshelves them.
Adding to Atlas' globe, they dispose themselves
with a fat propriety, and pose as garlands
importantly about his burdened shoulders.
Occasionally a lift of wind uncarves them.

Stone becomes them; they in their turn become it.
Their opal eyes have a monumental cast.
And, in a maze of noise,
their quiet *croomb croomb* dignifies the spaces,
suggesting the sound of silence. On cobbled islands,
marooned in tantrums of traffic, they know their place.
Faithful and anonymous, like servants,
they never beg, but properly receive.

Arriving in rainbows of oil-and-water feathers,
they fountain down from buttresses and outcrops,
from Fontainebleau and London,
and, perched on the margins of roofs, with a gargoyle look,
they note, from an edge of air, with hooded eyes,
the city slowly lessening the sky.

All praise to them who nightly in the parks
keep peace for us; who, cosmopolitan,
patrol and people all cathedraled places,
the paved courts of the past, pompous as keepers,
and easily, lazily haunt and inhabit
St. Paul's, St. Peter's, or the Madeleine—
a sober race of messengers and custodians,
neat in their international uniforms,
alighting with a word perhaps from Rome.
Permanence is their business, space and time

their special preservations; and wherever
the great stone men we save from death are stationed,
appropriately on the head of each is perched,
as though for ever, his appointed pigeon.

Weathering

I am old enough now for a tree
once planted, knee high, to have grown to be
twenty times me,

and to have seen babies marry, and heroes grow deaf—
but that's enough meaning-of-life.
It's living through time we ought to be connoisseurs of.

From wearing a face all this time, I am made aware
of the maps faces are, of the inside wear and tear.
I take to faces that have come far.

In my father's carved face, the bright eye
he sometimes would look out of, seeing a long way
through all the tree-rings of his history.

I am awed by how things weather: an oak mantel
in the house in Spain, fingered to a sheen,
the marks of hands leaned into the lintel,

the tokens in the drawer I sometimes touch—
a crystal lived-in on a trip, the watch
my father's wrist wore to a thin gold sandwich.

It is an equilibrium
which breasts the cresting seasons but still stays calm
and keeps warm. It deserves a good name.

Weathering. Patina, gloss, and whorl.
The trunk of the almond tree, gnarled but still fruitful.
Weathering is what I would like to do well.

Outlook, Uncertain

No season
brings conclusion.

Each year,
through heartache, nightmare,

true loves alter,
marriages falter,

and lovers illumine
the antique design,

apart, together,
foolish as weather,

right as rain,
sure as ruin.

Must you, then, and I
adjust the whole sky

over every morning?
Or else, submitting

to cloud and storm,
enact the same

lugubrious ending,
new lives pending?

James Bottle's Year

December finds him
outside, looking skyward.
The year gets a swearword.

His rage is never permanent.
By January he's out,
silent and plough-bent.

All white February,
he's in a fury
of wind-grief and ground-worry.

By March, he's back
scouring the ground for luck,
for rabbit-run and deer-track.

April is all sounds and smiles.
The hill is soft with animals.
His arms describe miles.

The local girls say
he's honeyed and bee-headed
at haytime in May.

In June,
he'll stay up late, he'll moon
and talk to children.

No one sees him in July.
At dawn, he'll ride away
with distance in his eye.

In August, you'd assume
yourself to be almost welcome.
He keeps open time.

But, on one September morning,
you'll see cloud-worries form.
His eyes flash storm warnings.

October is difficult.
He tries to puzzle out
if it's his or the season's fault.

In November, he keeps still
through hail and snowfall,
thinking through it all.

What's causing the odd weather?
Himself, or the capricious air?
Or the two together?

December, breathing hard,
he's back outside, hurling skyward
his same swearword.

Daedalus

My son has birds in his head.

I know them now. I catch
the pitch of their calls, their shrill
cacophonies, their chitterings, their coos.
They hover behind his eyes and come to rest
on a branch, on a book, grow still,
claws curled, wings furled.
His is a bird world.

I learn the flutter of his moods,
his moments of swoop and soar.
From the ground I feel him try
the limits of the air—
sudden lift, sudden terror—
and move in time to cradle
his quivering, feathered fear.

At evening, in the tower,
I see him to sleep and see
the hooding-over of eyes,
the slow folding of wings.
I wake to his morning twitterings,
to the *croomb* of his becoming.

He chooses his selves—wren, hawk,
swallow or owl—to explore
the trees and rooftops of his heady wishing.
Tomtit, birdwit.
Am I to call him down, to give him
a grounding, teach him gravity?
Gently, gently.
Time tells us what we weigh, and soon enough
his feet will reach the ground.
Age, like a cage, will enclose him.
So the wise men said.

My son has birds in his head.

The Fall

He teeters along the crumbling top
of the garden wall and calls, "Look up,
Papa, look up! I'm flying . . ." till,
in a sudden foreseen spasm, I see him fall.

Terrible
when fear cries to the senses, when the whirl
of the possible drowns the real. Falling
is a fright in me. I call
and move in time to catch
his small, sweat-beaded body,
still thrilled with the air.
"I flew, Papa, I flew!"
"I know, child, I know."

The Spiral

The seasons of this year are in my luggage.
Now, lifting the last picture from the wall,
I close the eyes of the room. Each footfall
clatters on the bareness of the stair.
The family ghosts fade in the hanging air.
Mirrors reflect the silence. There is no message.
I wait in the still hall for a car to come.
Behind, the house will dwindle to a name.

Places, addresses, faces left behind.
The present is a devious wind
obliterating days and promises.
Tomorrow is a tinker's guess.
Marooned in cities, dreaming of greenness,
or dazed by journeys, dreading to arrive—
change, change is where I live.

For possibility,
I choose to leave behind
each language, each country.
Will this place be an end,
or will there be one other,
truer, rarer?

Often now, in dream,
abandoned landscapes come,
figuring a constant theme:
Have you left us behind?
What have you still to find?

Across the spiral distance,
through time and turbulence,
the rooted self in me
maps out its true country.

And, as my father found
his own small weathered island,
so will I come to ground

where that small man, my son,
can put his years on.

For him, too, time will turn.

An Instance

Perhaps the accident of a bird
crossing the green window, a simultaneous phrase
of far singing, and a steeplejack
poised on the church spire, changing the gold clock,
set the moment alight. At any rate, a word
in that instant of realizing catches fire,
ignites another, and soon the page is ablaze
with a wildfire of writing. The clock chimes in the square.

All afternoon, in a scrawl of time,
the mood still smoulders. Rhyme remembers rhyme,
and words summon the moment when amazement
ran through the senses like a flame.
Later, the song forgotten, the sudden bird
flown who-knows-where, the incendiary word
long since crossed out, the steeplejack gone home,
their moment burns again, restored
to its spontaneity. The poem stays.

The O-Filler

One noon in the library, I watched a man—
imagine!—filling in O's, a little, rumpled
nobody of a man, who licked his stub of pencil
and leaned over every O with a loving care,
shading it neatly, exactly to its edges
until the open pages
were pocked and dotted with solid O's, like towns
and capitals on a map. And yet, so peppered,
the book appeared inhabited and complete.

That whole afternoon, as the light outside softened
and the library groaned woodenly,
he worked and worked, his o-so-patient shading
descending like an eyelid over each open O
for page after page. Not once did he miss one,
or hover even a moment over an *a*
or an *e* or a *p* or a *g*. Only the O's—
oodles of O's, O's multitudinous, O's manifold,
O's italic and roman.
And what light on his crumpled face when he discovered—
as I supposed—odd words like *zoo* and *ooze*,
polo, oolong and *odontology*!

Think now. In that limitless library,
all round the steep-shelved walls, bulging in their bindings,
books stood, waiting. Heaven knows how many
he had so far filled, but still there remained
uncountable volumes of O-laden prose, and odes
with inflated capital O's (in the manner of Shelley),
O-bearing Bibles and biographies,
even whole sections devoted to O alone,
all his for the filling. Glory, glory, glory!
How utterly open and endless the world must have seemed to him,
how round and ample! Think of it. A pencil
was all he needed. Life was one wide O.

And why, at the end of things, should O's not be closed
as eyes are? I envied him, for in my place
across the table from him, had I accomplished
anything as firm as he had, or as fruitful?
What could I show? A handful of scrawled lines,
an afternoon yawned and wondered away,
and a growing realization that in time
even my scribbled words would come
under his grubby thumb, and the blinds be drawn
on all my O's, with only this thought for comfort—
that when he comes to this poem, a proper joy
may amaze his wizened face and, o, a pure pleasure
make his meticulous pencil quiver.

A Lesson in Music

Play the tune again: but this time
with more regard for the movement at the source of it
and less attention to time. Time falls
curiously in the course of it.

Play the tune again: not watching
your fingering, but forgetting, letting flow
the sound till it surrounds you. Do not count
or even think. Let go.

Play the tune again: but try to be
nobody, nothing, as though the pace
of the sound were your heart beating, as though
the music were your face.

Play the tune again. It should be easier
to think less every time of the notes, of the measure.
It is all an arrangement of silence. Be silent, and then
play it for your pleasure.

Play the tune again; and this time, when it ends,
do not ask me what I think. Feel what is happening
strangely in the room as the sound glooms over
you, me, everything.

Now,
play the tune again.

Speaking a Foreign Language

How clumsy on the tongue, these acquired idioms,
after the innuendos of our own. How far
we are from foreigners, what faith
we rest in one sentence, hoping a smile will follow
on the appropriate face, always wallowing
between what we long to say and what we can,
trusting the phrase is suitable to the occasion,
the accent passable, the smile real,
always asking the traveler's fearful question—
what is being lost in translation?

Something, to be sure. And yet, to hear
the stumbling of foreign friends, how little we care
for the wreckage of word or tense. How endearing they are,
and how our speech reaches out, like a helping hand,
or limps in sympathy. Easy to understand,
through the tangle of language, the heart behind
groping toward us, to make the translation of
syntax into love.

Where Truth Lies

Maps, once made,
leave the impression of a place gone dead.

Words, once said,
anchor the swirlings in the head.

Vows, once taken,
waste in the shadows of a time forsaken.

Oh, understand
how the mind's landscape grows from shifting sand,

how where we are
is half on solid ground, half head-in-air,

a twilit zone
where changing flesh and changeless ghost are one,

and what is true
lies between you and the idea of you—

a friction,
restless, between the fact and the fiction.

WORDINGS

Scratch a poet and you will find, as often as not, a word-player, a puzzler, a palindromist, a punster, certainly someone bedazzled by language and addicted to exploring its astonishments and delights, those occasional felicities that Cyril Connolly called "unbreakable toys for the mind."

Mandala: Dilemma

Counters

ounce	instant
dice	distant
trice	tryst
quartz	catalyst
quince	quest
sago	sycamore
serpent	sophomore
oxygen	oculist
nitrogen	novelist
denim	dentist

acreage	archery
brokerage	butchery
cribbage	treachery
carthage	taproom
cage	tomb
sink	sermon
sentiment	cinnamon
ointment	apron
nutmeg	nunnery
doom	density

Palindrome

T. Eliot, top bard, notes putrid tang emanating, is sad. I'd assign it a
name: "Gnat dirt upset on drab pot toilet."

REVIEWS, ETC.

Throughout my long association with The New Yorker, *its extraordinary and much-loved editor, William Shawn, encouraged his writers mainly to follow their noses. This gave me the freedom to pursue my own curiosity, to write prose chronicles from different parts of the world, to review from time to time books for which I felt a special enthusiasm, to address subjects as diverse as gypsies and cricket, and to report on sporting occasions. A few of these writings follow.*

Ask for Nicolás Catari

S O M E H O W (and it would be worth someone's patient attention to work out just why), Latin America remains curiously fictive in the Western mind—in the minds, at least, of those who have never been driven, out of curiosity or circumstance, to find out about it. Perhaps "filmic" would be a better word than "fictive"—the image of Latin America in the popular consciousness seems to stem from a mixture of Carmen Miranda, Cantinflas, and the cha-cha-cha, with a script that veers from Woody Allen banana republic to Montezuma-sized epic. For the British, the continent has an aura of remote geography lessons, which is where I first met it—always the least pawed page in the atlas. It was only when I lived in Spain that Latin America began to take on substance, as the New World. Traditionally, older Spaniards have much the same attitude toward the Latin American countries as the more unbending English toward the United States ("Tell me, is it true that in the United States one lunches at the chemist's?"), but in Spain I talked with real Latin Americans—or real Peruvians and Chileans and Colombians, rather, for Latin America is something of a geographical myth—and eventually, in a series of journeys there, I learned the extent of my ignorance, and have been chipping away at it ever since. In the course of conversations about Latin America, however, I still find myself having to draw maps in the air. The geography of the continent gets in the way of its humanity: people know infinitely less about the character of Venezuelans and Bolivians than they do about Serbs and Croats or the peoples of the Middle East. And if one uses the term "Latin America" correctly—to embrace the Spanish-, Portuguese-, and French-speaking countries of the South American continent, Central America, and the Caribbean—the physical, political, and cultural complexity of such

181

a mess of national entities looks too forbidding to disentangle, and the continent is left in shadow, on the fringes of serious attention.

One solid piece of reassurance comes to me annually, in the form of *The South American Handbook*, a publication that goes a long way to bringing Latin America into the light. It has had a singular evolution: it began in 1921 as a fairly sketchy guide for British businessmen going "out" to that continent, and, apart from a few wartime gaps, it has appeared every December since, in an ever-fattening form; the 1977 edition is the fifty-third. The *Handbook* was originally put together by the Federation of British Industries and later backed by British shipping interests, which were then powerfully connected to Latin America. Six years ago, when these business interests withdrew their support and it looked as if publication might cease, the *Handbook* was taken over by the printing firm that produced it, Dawson & Goodall, in Bath, in the West of England—as well-groomed and un-Latin-American a place as there is. Its thousand-odd pages of small and busy print clamor for the attention of anyone who is keen on armchair travel or is thirsty for sheer information.

Curiously, *The South American Handbook* remains almost unknown except to a small and passionate band of initiates who have traveled in Latin America in its company, and who, as a result, stay loyal to it forever, and can usually recite chosen passages by heart. In the 1950s, the *Handbook* began asking its readers to correct its information from the field, and now it draws on a flood of correspondence for factual information and a whimsically varying prose manner. With such meticulous help from its correspondents, the *Handbook* updates itself every year, even to prices, which, given certain Latin American inflation rates, can change out of all recognition. (The price of a rented hammock at the Mayan ruins of Tikal is still fifty cents, however.) Taking each country in turn, the *Handbook* moves pyramidally from the general to the particular: from geographical and historical summations to regions, cities, towns, and even villages, from current economic reports to a concluding section of brisk practical information on matters like money, travel, documents, food, dress, and national habits, sufficient to allay the anxieties of even the most timorous.

The pleasure one takes in reading the *Handbook* is that of feeling the huge, unwieldy abstractions of the Latin American countries reduced to a sharply observed particularity, as though they had been trudged through by someone in no hurry at all, and taken in by a kindly, unjudging, sympathetic eye. It has none of the lapel-tugging tone of those trailblazing guides written for tourists, and treats its readers, instead, as travelers who are out to see and absorb. It proffers its occasional advice with a nannylike, finger-wagging directness, even reminding us where certain church services are conducted in English. But it will quite often turn either wry or lyrical where the circumstance seems to demand it.

Soaked in attention, the little crowded capsule of the *Handbook* swells into a whole continent of information. I cannot think of any better way of illustrating the arbitrary richness of this prodigious vade mecum than by stitching together a random patchwork of some of its entries, ranging from the blunt to the exotic. Sanity is its keynote, and its temper remains unruffled in the face of the most improbable trials:

> Be careful when asking directions. Many Latin Americans will give you the wrong answer rather than admit they do not know; this may be partly because they fear losing face, but is also because they like to please!

But the dry editorial smile is never too far from the surface:

> Chagas' Disease (South American Trypanosomiasis) is a chronic illness, incurable, transmitted by the "barber bug," which lives in rural districts on dirt floors frequented by opossums. It bites at night so avoid sleeping in such conditions.

> If you are unlucky enough to be bitten by a venomous snake, spider, scorpion or sea creature, always try (within limits) to catch the animal for identification.

> In reply to our 1972 statement that some State Tourist Hotels [in Peru] find the proper tariff too difficult to calculate and charge a blanket 12%, the Tourist Department emphatically deny that there is any surcharge for extra blankets at any of their hotels.

> In this Sierra [in Colombia] live the Motilones Indians. A connoisseur of the ironies of history will know that at the Congress of El Rosario one of the items most acclaimed was the admission of aboriginal Indians into citizenship. The Motilones have always turned a blind eye to this, for they are the only Indians in Colombia who have refused to accept the inevitable.

Little is known of them, for so far they have persisted in killing many of the missionaries sent to Christianize them, and the anthropologists sent to study them.

The great achievement of the *Handbook*—and it comes largely from the practice of using the material sent in by enthusiastic travelers—is that of bringing Latin America into the focus of individual perception. Entries like the following have a certain endearing practicality to them:

On the Bolivian side, in Lake Huanamarca, i.e. from Straits of Tiquina south, the best way to visit the Lake from La Paz is to take from Avenida Buenos Aires a bus to Huatajata and there ask for Nicolás Catari. He is a great boat-builder and knows the Lake well.

Similarly:

If the Bolivian Immigration Officer at Villazón is not in his office, you can ask for him at Hotel Panamericano, just up from the Post Office.

Its practicality is often laconically direct:

1st class US$4.50, 2nd US$2.50, no apparent difference.

Clearly, the *Handbook* has the traveler's welfare at heart, warning like a wise uncle against pitfalls and pickpockets, but without any pious moralizing:

During the new year's fiesta [in Pasto, Colombia] there is a "Día de los Negros" on Jan. 5 and a "Día de los Blancos" next day. On "black day" people dump their hands in black grease and paint, without exception, each other's faces black. On "white day" they throw talc or flour at each other. Local people wear their oldest clothes. Things can get quite violent. On December 28 and Feb. 5, there is also a "Fiesta de las Aguas" when anything that moves—only tourists, because locals know better—gets drenched with water from balconies and even from fire engines' hoses.

Visitors should know—for their own good—that a thriving industry in Quito is the production of religious paintings of a medieval type. And another is the stealthy sale by dubious chaps of shrunken heads (*tsantsa*), war trophies of the Jivaro head-hunters. Nowadays they are fakes made out of goatskin, their long black hair making them look very like the real thing.

I was able to test the following advice, and, in consequence, I would never dream of ignoring the *Handbook*'s counsel:

184

On the night ferry to Montevideo rush to the dining place if you want to spare yourself a supperless night.

And think of the difference the following information makes to a traveler in the Central Cordillera region of Colombia:

The gardens, and even the stations, are bright with flowers. The track, however, leaves much to be desired and always seems to be under repair; the journey by rail takes 24 hours whereas buses do it in seven.

I find myself hoping that the countries in question take heed of the *Handbook*, for they might be able to do something about a comment like this:

You need to have your own shoe-cleaning equipment; there seem to be no shoeshine boys in any of the Guianas!

And my favorite warning of all, which must make anyone wary of ever opening his mouth in Guatemala:

Watch out for would-be guides in Antigua who engage you in friendly conversation and then charge you US$3 for the privilege.

It is impossible to wander in the *Handbook* without amassing a treasury of miscellaneous information, which is usually delivered as a murmured aside:

[In Potosí, Bolivia] immense amounts of silver were once extracted from this hill. In Spain, "*éste es un Potosí*" ("it's a Potosí") is still used for anything superlatively rich.

In Gualeguay, Argentina:

The house from whose ridgepole Garibaldi was hung by one hand and tortured by the local chief of police in 1837, in the time of Rosas, still exists.

And a rich nugget of information about Nevis, in the Leeward Islands:

Here Nelson met and married Frances Nesbit; the Nesbit plantation still exists today and is a guest house open all the year round (US$40 single, MAP). Here, too, was born Alexander Hamilton, who helped to draft the American Constitution. The former capital, Jamestown, was drowned by a tidal wave in 1680. The submerged town can still be visited by snorkellers and skindivers and, according to the locals, the tolling of its church bells can still be heard.

It is, however, the occasional sentences cropping up suddenly in the brisk summations of landscapes and small towns which will startle a scene or an atmosphere into being, scattered like jewels in the text and reading as though they might have fallen from the prose of some of the Latin American novelists:

Vultures still stalk the streets like turkeys.

The ruins are vestigial; the cacti are far more interesting.

Now and then the drab, depressing landscape is brightened by the red poncho of an Indian shepherd watching his sheep.

From there, is a road through Panzós to Tactic, which is famous for beautiful *huipiles* and for its "living well," in which the water becomes agitated as one approaches.

The streets, steep, twisted and narrow, follow the contour of the hills and are sometimes steps cut into the rock: one, the Street of the Kiss, is so narrow that kisses can be—and are—exchanged from opposite balconies.

West of Tandil stood the famous balancing stone called the Piedra Movediza; it fell of its own accord in 1912. Whilst it stood, the huge mass of granite was so exquisitely balanced that light puffs of wind would set it swaying. Indians in the last century believed the stone would fall as a sign of God's approbation if white men were driven out of the country. General Rosas ordered the stone to be pulled down, but a number of men hauling away with oxen teams failed to dislodge it.

A large number of Indians are met on the road: peripatetic merchants laden with goods, or villagers driving pigs to market, or women carrying babies and cockerels and fruits. Your driver can usually tell from their costumes where they come from. The merchant will often do a round of 200 km. and make no more than a dollar or two, but he likes wandering, the contacts with strange people and the novel sights. He pleases himself, pleases his customers and . . . is not much concerned whether he can make pleasure pay.

One has to be grateful for good guidebooks—their compressed experience saves a lot of time. Wandering about in Latin America with the comfortable bulk of *The South American Handbook* has led me to feel the greatest possible respect for its English good sense, its crisp practicality, its gentle curiosity. It is English, too, in its political imperviousness: whatever horrors and injustices may be enacted in these territories, the territories are at least there.

The Giant Ground Sloth
and Other Wonders

SINCE TOURISTS took over from travelers, the times have not been kind to those few, rare writers who have always seen the world well for us—who filter unknown landscapes through the screen of their curiosity, who travel at a human pace, and who keep notes that allow us to take armchair journeys after them. Now even the waste places of the world are discovered regularly for us by documentary camera crews, and the records of articulate, lone travelers have given way to anonymous guidebooks, which list what to see and where to eat, drink, sleep, and be gratified in varying degrees of comfort. The unknown looks sometimes like a beaten track.

The English, perhaps because they look on strangenesses with a piercingly cool eye, have turned up a steady stream of enlightening travelers, from Doughty and Stevenson, through Lawrence, Huxley, V. S. Pritchett, and Graham Greene, to Lawrence Durrell, Laurie Lee, and Patrick Leigh Fermor. But such writings have dwindled over the last two decades, giving way to more massive studies, which sum up countries and tell us everything about them except what they are like. Lawrence Durrell's Corfu, which he re-created so richly and strangely in his many-layered *Prospero's Cell*, in 1945, has now fallen afoul of tourism, and even the square white house in the northeast of the island where Durrell wrote the book has a place on the tourist itinerary. Yet there are endless alluring unknowns, lacking only a traveler with time to take them in, with an uncommitted curiosity and an unjudging eye, and with an appropriate prose manner. These qualities come brilliantly together in Bruce Chatwin, whose *In Patagonia* takes traveling back to its magic roots. Speaking of his book, Mr. Chatwin has this to say:

> *In Patagonia* is not a travel book in the usual sense, but a Quest or Wonder Voyage. It is about wandering and exile, and its structure is as old

as literature itself: the narrator travels to a remote country in search of a strange beast and, as he goes along, describes his encounters with other people whose stories delay him en route.

Mr. Chatwin is as good as his word. He remains rigorously true to the tradition of the traveler's tale—the oldest form of storytelling—and never once intrudes himself self-consciously into the narrative. We know nothing about him at the book's end except that he has been ears, eyes, and memory to us—not impersonal but unpersonal. He is less a traveler than a wanderer, for he has few express intentions. His journey, through the startling landscapes of Patagonia and Tierra del Fuego, is thoroughly externalized, in sharp physical detail. He has the power of compressing place and character into small and vivid compass:

It stopped raining and I came to leave, Bees hummed around the poet's hives. His apricots were ripening the color of a pale sun. Clouds of thistle-down drifted across the view and in a field there were some fleecy white sheep.

Three ancient Scots stood by. Their eyes were bloodshot-pink and nursery-blue and their teeth worn to little brown pinnacles.

The wind had polished his nose and coloured it pale lilac. I found him at lunch ladling the borscht into the ivory orb of his head. He had made his room cheerful, in the Baltic way, with flowered curtains, geraniums, diplomas for stunt flying and a signed photograph of Neil Armstrong. All his books were in Lithuanian, the aristocrat of Indo-European languages, and concerned his country's plans for independence.

The day before I had met the nuns of the Santa María Auxiliadora Convent on their Saturday coach outing to the penguin colony on Cabo Vírgenes. A bus-load of virgins. Eleven thousand virgins. About a million penguins. Black and white. Black and white. Black and white.

These clear-cut cameos seem almost surreal separated from the thread of the narrative, but so do the scenes and characters in the book, for they loom like outposts of human existence against the empty landscape of the Patagonian desert. Since Patagonia has been settled largely in this century, the figures that Mr. Chatwin meets (Welsh, Scots, English, Boers, French, Russians, Germans, Yugoslavs, Arabs, Persians even) have come from other lives, each with the tale of a journey, and the encounters become small inset narratives—as do tracks of history, for the past intrudes regularly as anecdote and memory into the journey. Mr. Chatwin intrudes, too, his own sudden connections: brooding on the derivation of the name Patagonia, he brushes aside the accepted version (from the Spanish *patacones*, or "big feet"), lights on the Greek word πάταγος, meaning "roaring," and turns up a chivalric romance called "Primaleon of Greece," published in Castile in 1512, seven years before Magellan's voyage of discovery, which mentions a roaring monster called the Grand Patagon. He goes on to suppose that Shakespeare, who read a contemporary account of Magellan's voyage—during which Magellan had attempted to imprison some of the half-tamed Patagonian natives—must have used it as the source for Caliban. Mr. Chatwin is as close to travelers' tales of the past and to the travelers whose paths he is crossing as he is to the landscape and its present inhabitants. What he shares with all of them is a sense of strangeness on the earth's surface, an awed sense of separation from anything fixed. He even sets himself up with a mock quest as a whimsical excuse for his journey. During his English childhood, his grandmother kept as a sacred relic a piece of what she insisted was brontosaurus skin, with coarse red hairs, brought back from Patagonia by her cousin, a sea captain called Charley Milward. It was unceremoniously thrown out on her death, but it serves Mr. Chatwin as a kind of Grail. The brontosaurus turns out to have been a mylodon, or giant ground sloth, and toward the end of the book, following Charley Milward's trail, Mr. Chatwin makes his way to a cave near Last Hope Sound, in Chile, where he finds some familiar coarse red hairs. His journey is toward the enfabled Patagonia of his childhood.

Patagonia suits Mr. Chatwin admirably well, given his disposition toward wonders, both past and present. It is virtually only since 1877, when sheep farming was profitably introduced, that the region has attracted settlers from various parts of Europe, and their remote stations are often repositories of a pre-Patagonian existence. Each case of exile is a different story, entered into for distinct reasons, and each of the characters who punctuate the journey is an incarnation of a separate past. Mr. Chatwin's first encounter is in Paris, prior to the journey, with His Royal Highness Prince Philippe of Araucania and Patagonia, a descendant of the self-proclaimed kings of Patagonia, and very nearly a parody of pretenders. In the province of Chubut,

Mr. Chatwin comes across the descendants of Welsh settlers who fled
the restrictive life of Wales to found, in 1865, a colony where Welsh
customs still prevail and where the Welsh language is, improbably,
still spoken. Throughout this Patagonian journey, there are many
images of national transplanting: hymn singing in a Welsh chapel
in the middle of a Patagonian field with a storm raging outside; tea
in Punta Arenas with a dauntless old Chilean-Scottish lady whose
farm was stripped from her during the Allende years; an interlude
with a Scottish sheep farmer who carves his own bagpipes; veiled
accounts of the male witches of Chiloé Island. And Mr. Chatwin
runs with reliable regularity into traces of legendary figures: Butch
Cassidy and the Sundance Kid, who lit out for Patagonia in 1901, and
whose legend still exists there in variant forms; the many voyages
of his ancestor Charley Milward; the surveying journeys of H. M. S.
Beagle to Tierra del Fuego, which inspire Mr. Chatwin to tell once
again the amazing story of the Tierra del Fuegan Jemmy Button, who
was taken to England by Captain Robert Fitzroy and, after acquir-
ing the trappings of civilization, was brought back on the Beagle's
second voyage (the one that carried the young Darwin) to revert to
his native existence, eventually turning brutally on those who had at-
tempted to civilize him. The story of Jemmy Button has been told by
many hands—most notably by a Chilean novelist, the late Benjamin
Subercaseaux—and surely cries out to be a film of epic proportions.
It reminds Mr. Chatwin of Poe and his "Narrative of Arthur Gordon
Pym." This propensity to make sudden, surprising connections, to
follow clues, keeps us as readers on the keen edge of anticipation.

In Patagonia jogs us with the realization that what we have come
to regard as travel is no more than geographical transference, where
hardly anything changes, where map and guidebook obliterate the
landscape, where journeys are taken for the purpose of summing up,
of reaching a conclusion—the very opposite of a wonder voyage. The
book is of infinitely more value than cheap air fares. Mr. Chatwin's
prose is honed to bare and moving essentials. The following gnomic
exchange may serve as a concentrated example:

"How much was the room?"
"Nothing. If you hadn't slept in it, nobody else would."
"How much was dinner?"
"Nothing. How could we know you were coming? We cooked for our-
selves."

"Then how much was the wine?"

"We always give wine to visitors."

"What about the maté?"

"Nobody pays for maté."

"What can I pay for then? There's only bread and coffee left."

"I can't charge you for bread, but café au lait is a gringo drink and I shall make you pay."

Immortal Diamond

WITH ADMIRABLE INSISTENCE, the Ecco Press reissued, under the heading Neglected Books of the Twentieth Century, *The Diary of "Helena Morley,"* edited and translated by Elizabeth Bishop. The book previously appeared in 1957, and I hope that this time round it will put its neglect behind it, for I cannot think of a journal that approaches it in its exuberant appetite for daily existence. It is a diary that was kept by a young girl in the town of Diamantina, in Brazil, between 1893 and 1895—from her twelfth to her fifteenth year—and that, even at such a remove of time, goes on happening in its own enclosed and detailed present.

We are lucky to have Helena Morley's diary at all, since it was a spontaneous creation, never intended to see the light as a historical document, or even as a book. In her preface to the modest, privately printed first edition, published in Rio de Janeiro in 1942, the author, who was then in her sixties, explained its coming into being:

> When I was a child my father encouraged me to form the habit of writing down everything that happened to me. Almost every day at school the Portuguese teacher expected us to write a composition, which could be a description, a letter, or an account of what we had been doing. I found it was easiest to write about myself and my very numerous family. These compositions, filling many notebooks and loose sheets, were hidden away for years and years and forgotten. Finally I began to go over them and arrange them for my own family, chiefly for my granddaughters. It was their idea, to which I consented, to make a book that might show the girls of today the differences between present-day life and the simple existence we led at that time.

The book's reputation spread in Brazil by what John Osborne has called "the blessed alchemy of word of mouth," and it was reprinted several times by demand, receiving the enthusiastic blessing of Georges Bernanos, then an exile in Brazil, and attracting a cult of evangelistic readers. It has, of course, the advantage of all journals, that of growing more interesting with time; but *The Diary of "Helena Morley"* (the pseudonym comes from the English side of her family, her grandfather having been an English doctor to mining communities who remained in Brazil for his health) has a quality far beyond the documentary, rich in domestic detail though it is. It happens to contain, in the darting, delighted pace of its writing, both a loving eye for human quirks and an enviable equilibrium between self and place.

What we, as readers of English, have to be grateful for is Elizabeth Bishop's devotion, as editor and as translator. In a long introduction to her 1957 translation, she described how when she first lived in Brazil her friends pressed the book on her, and how her increasing delight in it became a decision to translate it. But she did so much more than render the book into English. Discovering that Helena Morley was living in Rio, she arranged to meet her, and gives a rather eerie account of those meetings, for the exuberant schoolgirl was then a matron of seventy-six, something like the revered grandmother of the diary. It is an odd experience for any translator to meet the author he is translating, across languages; but this was stranger still, for Elizabeth Bishop was meeting the girl author of the diary across time as well. Miss Bishop undertook, in addition, a journey to Diamantina, one of the highest towns in Brazil, and reports on the appearance of the place with the double vision of Helena's written perspective and her own, identifying familiar buildings and generally laying the text against reality. Out of the conversations she had about Diamantina's past with people there, some of whom had figured in the diary in younger versions, she fills in for us the raw elements of Helena's Diamantina—practical notes on food and prices, and conditions of work in the diamond mines, where Helena's wise father scratched for an up-and-down living. Such a journey to the physical reality behind the text can only sharpen a translation, and make it more than a matter of an equivalence in language. So Miss Bishop's introduction creates a separately fascinating setting for the text; and when in this reissue of the book she adds a short foreword noting the death of the author we have an odd sense of frames within frames, of looking down a well at the bottom of which gleams the diary itself.

In translation, Helena becomes neither English nor American but remains her quick-witted Brazilian self, so well has Elizabeth Bishop caught her tone, the chirping of adolescent curiosity, the breathless switches of attention, the flit from one emotion to another. It might be assumed that any bright child, given the encouragement that Helena had to keep a journal, could produce a readable account of three years anywhere. Here I am inclined to agree with Georges Bernanos when, in a letter written to the author in 1945, he refers to her diary as "one of those books, so rare in any literature, that owe nothing to either experience or talent, but everything to *ingenium*, to genius—for we should not be afraid of that much misused word—to genius drawn from its very source, to the genius of adolescence." There is nothing in the least secretive or confessional about *The Diary of "Helena Morley."* The writing of it appears for her a natural act, an overflowing of her energetic attention. She enjoys her journal as she enjoys her many chores; it pleases her beloved father and amuses her family, and it serves her as an agreeable alternative to imposed homework. Daily happenings, the members of her many-layered family, local characters, her own moods and occasional idiocies she externalizes with an easy frankness, and she has a sharp ear for the adult conversations she is always eavesdropping on, and for family stories, which she heard, after all, over and over again. Her family is the center of her known world, the reality she embraces, and her occasional speculative musings always take flight from some domestic incident, as when, faced with the family ironing, she sighs for simpler days:

> I began to iron a dress with ruffles and I got to thinking that so much work was ridiculous, that we should just wear baize skirts the way they used to in the old days.
> So I spent the afternoon without doing anything. Because I'm never too lazy to write, I'm going to write down here a story of the old days, for the future, as papa says. Who knows if in the future there won't be many more inventions than there are today? José Rabelo spends his time weighing vultures on the scales, in order to invent a flying-machine. Wouldn't that be wonderful! Sometimes I feel envious when I see the vultures soaring up so high. How would it be if I could turn into a vulture? It would be awfully funny. But it would be better to discover something so that people wouldn't die. However, until we can fly, as José says we're going to be able to, it would be better to go back to the old days and wear baize or cotton skirts! What a good idea!
> Grandma talks about the life she led in Lomba and I get so envious of

her! If they wanted to write they caught a goose, pulled out a wing-feather, and made a point at the end.

In 1893, when Helena began her diary, it was not yet five years since Dom Pedro the Second had abolished slavery in Brazil, and hardly three since the proclamation of the Brazilian Republic. Yet Helena's Diamantina is so much an outpost, so work-committed and so self-dependent, that the outside world scarcely intrudes at all, except as occasional visitors or elections, each of which is prized by Helena as a diversion, for it is diversions she longs for and lives by, whether they be birthdays, holy days, sickness, or even death:

> In Diamantina a long sickness is more like a *festa* than anything else. We, that is all the cousins, like to make sick-calls as much as making novenas. Seu Vieira's sickness has been a great distraction. One of my friends has already got engaged making sick-calls there. He's been sick for a month now, but dying for only a week.

Her sense of her own self, her difference, she touches on only in passing, like a hummingbird:

> I'm almost fourteen years old and already I think more than all the rest of the family. I think I began to draw conclusions from the age of ten years, or less. And I swear I never saw anybody from mama's family think about things. They hear something and believe it; and that's that for the rest of their lives.
> They're all happy like that!

We are used to perceptive re-creations of adolescence in fiction; but, as Elizabeth Bishop underlines in her introduction, the things in Helena Morley's diary *did* happen, and that makes for a difference in our attention. We measure fictional re-creations against the real, after all, and Helena's written high spirits give us one such authentic measure. She does not stop often to think about the act of writing, for to her it is as natural a chore as washing the clothes in the river or guddling for diamonds. But when she does she makes mock of writers' blocks, and, indeed, of writing as a self-conscious act:

> I was sitting, pen in hand, trying to think of something to write, because nothing's happened for days. It's rained all week; today's the first fine day. I went to the window to see if by looking at the sky and the stars something would come to me. Nothing. A funeral went by, coming up from Rio Grande. I thought: Will that give me a subject? No, because I don't know who it is.

I turned around, thinking I'd just copy the exercise from *Ornaments of Memory*, and tell the teacher tomorrow that I hadn't had time for the composition. When I turned around I saw mama, very annoyed with my brothers, who were sound asleep, struggling to get them on their feet while the corpse went by. I went through the same thing when I was little. I was pleased, because I'd found a subject.

And she remarks, rather indulgently, of her beloved grandmother:

She's very intelligent, but she never learned to read and write well and so she still thinks it's something almost supernatural to write things down with a pen. The funny thing is that she isn't impressed when I tell her things. It's because she thinks writing is so much more difficult.

It is a lucky book.

Inside Information

W H I L E   I   W A S growing up in Scotland, we were often visited in the country by an egg-bald, red-faced Uncle Charlie, who always brought us some bizarre gift—a Norwegian flag, a single spur— and gave off an atmosphere of what I retrospectively realize was whisky. But I remember him most vividly for something else entirely, for the inadvertent gift of a language. One time at table, Uncle Charlie's stomach rumbled royally. Winking at me and rolling his eyes, he glanced down affectionately and whispered to us, "That's the boys below the belt. They're always fighting." All at once, we saw the guerrilla bands swarming across the pink canyons of Uncle Charlie's interior. Our fairly bewildered view of our bodies changed at a stroke, for we suddenly had been given a way of talking about the mysterious processes going on inside us. If Uncle Charlie's stomach acted up with unusual violence, he would glare at it and mutter, "If you fellows are going to move that grand piano, at least pick it up!" He peopled our insides for us with an entourage of miniature staff members—kitchen and scullery maids who sloshed about the digestive tract in gum boots, teams of hardhats and crane drivers who manned the muscles, soft-footed librarians who prowled through the bookshelves in our heads, busy operators at the switchboard of the senses, nurses, scuba divers, commandos, and singing waiters. We turned what went on inside us into legend, and I have never quite lost the habit—I still think of myself as something rather like a stray ocean liner, kept afloat by a cantankerous knockabout crew.

I invoke Uncle Charlie because he did provide us children for a time with a serviceable metaphor. His whimsical anthropomorphizing allowed us at least to envision what was otherwise beyond us. My mother was a doctor, and would occasionally give us pocket lectures, usually at table, on matters like digestion, but her crisp explanations were nothing like as gripping as Uncle Charlie's accounts of barroom brawls in the small intestine. She talked, as doctors still do, about "the body," yet we had to take her on trust, because the insides were something she had seen and we had not. Our bodies may have been objects to her, but they were very much more to us who inhabited them and were often at their mercy.

The most woeful lack in our general education continues to be a working knowledge of what is going on inside us. The current flood of manuals on body awareness surely demonstrates how much we both lack and need an intelligent oneness with our physical selves. For all the advances in medical science, we remain remarkably naïve. Medical knowledge has not been translated into the language of general awareness. The chasm between the language of medical practitioners and that of laymen has not been crossed. We suspect doctors of obfuscation, but they probably tell us as best they can, as far as available language allows.

By coincidence, two books appear that address themselves to this very state of affairs—one by a doctor and one by a layman. From opposite sides of the fence, they set out to take stock of our connection with our bodies and to adjust our ordinary ignorance. Dr. Jonathan Miller's *The Body in Question* is a book of such compressed and essential insight that it should be soaked in water and studied at great length. It offers both doctors and laymen a wonderfully fresh look at the history of medicine. The body image is paradoxical, because "you cannot experience your own interior by closing your eyes and concentrating on it." Dr. Miller writes. "In order to discover your own contents you have to investigate the inside of someone else." For Dr. Miller, the advancement of medical knowledge has been synonymous with the coming into being of a language adequate and intricate enough to describe complex processes, often not observable. "The suspicion that [man's] effectiveness or agency was caused by something other than his conscious urge to be effective, and that he himself had no real control over this, constitutes an almost inconceivable leap of the imagination, and one can only conclude that it was largely the result of drawing an analogy between himself and his own technological artefacts." Medical science is not simply a specialized body of accumulated information but the cautious evolution of a way of thinking. Dr. Miller's book abounds in brilliant example: "One can only assume that Galen's inability [in the second century A.D.] to see the heart as a pump was due to the fact that such machines did not become a significant part of the cultural scene until long after his death." Medical science, far from advancing at a regular pace, has been encumbered by misunderstanding; Dr. Miller points out that "medicine did not make an effective contribution to human welfare until the middle of the twentieth century."

It is not until we come on a metaphor accurate and precise enough to convey an intricate physiological process—as, say, the analogy of the firing pin accurately conveys nerve–muscle stimulation—that we are able to understand that process fully, Dr. Miller suggests. "Nowadays, the process of perception and the method of science are both seen to depend on making creative conjectures about the nature of reality, and upon testing and remodelling these fictions until they self-evidently coincide with the outlines of the world's facts." Dr. Miller is his own best example, for his book crackles with crisp analogy and robust common sense. He is the perfect interpreter, in a context where explanations have conspicuously lacked sensible and intelligent translation.

The Body in Question is the residual text of Dr. Miller's much applauded BBC television series. Its television origins are retained in the form of lavish, wittily captioned illustrations, which crowd the book but, unfortunately, distract from the text. In his "Beyond the Fringe" days, Dr. Miller was for me the funniest man who trod the earth, and he has gone on to become the most vivid of "communicators." I think his text still needs him, wagging his finger from time to time, for it has a kind of breathless compression to it. It is, in a sense, the book of the movie, and I think it can only gain from being fleshed out by Dr. Miller himself.

"I live with this body of mine, and yet for all I know about it, I might be living with a stranger." In his *Living with a Stranger*, John Stewart Collis sets out resolutely to write about the body from the point of view of a puzzled occupant, and his insistent curiosity, his infectious astonishment make his book a joy to read. It begins in ignorance and ends in awe. He asks determinedly naïve questions, and patiently brings back answers from his extensive reading (his bibliography is a study in itself) and from the informed friends he claims to have pestered for explanations—for he is bent on understanding and will not be fobbed off with mere information. Geoffrey Grigson once wrote, "Hydrogen and oxygen may make up the water of life, but neither one by itself is a very satisfying drink." Mr. Collis would agree. He sets out on a systematic progress through human physiology, putting the body together as a living entity through an exploration of its constituent parts and processes. His chapters are wandering meditations on the parts and functions of the body, and are abundant in instance, anecdote, and ranging quotations. He is as aware as Dr. Miller of the necessity for metaphor in talking about the body, but he is not restricted by the need for the same precision and accuracy, and his figures are what we might call illuminations: "Though teeth seem as hard as marble, they are as frail as flowers." Putting the body into language at all is something of a restriction. "I do not think that words are adequate instruments for holding up the mirror to the nervous system," he writes, "nor do I favor pictorial presentation when too often we are presented with something resembling a horse's tail (at the lumbar region) rather than the actuality of the axionic and dentrical complex which is yet the definition of harmony. . . . It is only the imagination that can brood with any degree of insight upon the play of millions of cells and fibres acting and reacting in co-operative groups to promote, night and day whether we are awake or asleep, the common wealth of our metabolism." His determination to make the findings of medical science humanly comprehensible gives his book its freshness and originality. It is a rambling prose poem on the body, designed to awake in us an appropriate astonishment at our physical existence, to restore to the facts of science the awe they occasion in him.

Face to face with what he discovers about the body, Mr. Collis is resolutely awestruck. Existence to him is holy. This is the same disposition he brought to the natural world in his previous book, *The Worm Forgives the Plough*. In it, he quoted from John de Dondis, a fourteenth-century sage: "We are born and placed among wonders and surrounded by them, so that to whatever object the eye first turns, the same is wonderful and full of wonders, if only we will examine it for a while." He refuses to allow us to take the physical world, and the body in particular, for granted. In *Living with a Stranger*, he invokes the Goethe of Eckermann's *Gespräche*: "Awe is the highest thing in man; and if the pure phenomena awaken awe in him he should be content; he can be aware of nothing higher and should seek nothing beyond: here is the limit." Mr. Collis's humanism might seem old-fashioned, yet he makes it contagiously new in his manner, in the aura of profound joy that hangs over his writing. There is only one of him.

These books gain a great deal from being read together, for, however divergent their wavelengths, they are both invigorating restatements; they are both out to jolt us free of ingrained habits of thought, ingrained indifference. What I like to imagine, as I often do with books, is a conversation between their authors. I wish Uncle Charlie could eavesdrop on that hypothetical occasion. The librarians in his head would almost certainly take the day off to listen.

Heavy Breathing

I K N O W S O M E people who take not even a passing interest in sporting events of any kind, and who toss aside the sports sections of newspapers unread. I wonder at them—it is to me like ignoring a whole alternative universe, with its own laws, its own time scale, its own ethos, and its own history, a universe I have inhabited most of my life, and one my interest at least still inhabits. It is not to be confused with the real world, but it very often is. Jorge Luis Borges, in one of his best stories, "The Lottery of Babylon," projects a situation in which the people of his reconstructed Babylon, bored with the rational equanimity of their society, introduce, for the sake of diversion, a public lottery, repudiating their reality and replacing it with an arbitrary, constructed system of chance and thrill. The lottery gradually obsesses them, and drives them to add the possibility of losing and being penalized to that of winning, as an extra excitement. Borges clearly had Argentina and its national lottery in mind, but for me the story has certain inescapable sporting implications. As Borges' Babylon rejected the actual world for an invented one, so do we keep pulling sporting situations and events over our heads, and thriving on their expectations and satisfactions, which keep us fizzing from week to week, whatever else may be occurring in the real world.

*

I was initiated early, perched on my father's shoulders on a cold Saturday afternoon in Scotland, watching the bruising, grunting entanglement of a rugby scrum giving off exhausted breath in clouds and going nowhere. I could not understand the point of it, of course, but it was obviously of such passionate importance to the roaring men around me and the dying men on the field that it lodged itself indelibly in my head. I had never seen grown men behave like that before, and I felt I was being admitted to some secret rite—and, I suppose, I was. When my fellow-initiates and I began to play our own games, we never bothered about understanding the point or the rules; in fact, we hardly bothered about the ball, except as a prop. Instead, we put on elaborate mimes, in which we reenacted movements and gestures we had watched, down to the very grunts. I notice the same thing in public parks today, where undersized boys who have not yet learned to play show themselves to be already masters of all the theatricality of sport.

*

I had no idea then that I was entering a kind of tunnel; nor could I have guessed where it would lead. I have read more than my share of memoirs in which sensitive, game-hating schoolboys suffered at the hands of brutish, muscle-minded sports masters for their incompetence on the playing field; but for my own part I looked on games at school as pure liberation. Once out to grass, we were beyond the jurisdiction of teachers, independent of them, performers rather than apprentices. *We* were playing the game; teachers were excluded by their size. Nor did it occur to us that playing games had anything to do with forming our characters, although we quickly realized that playing them well would get us free time, attention, scholastic office, perhaps, and a certain official indulgence. What I remember most, however—what mattered most—was the pure physical pleasure of the game, whichever game it was: the endless moment when the ball would seem to stay at the top of its arc, suspended, before it began to fall back earthward, into the panting scramble below. Such moments were epiphanies. I was always playing something, and I did not particularly care which game it was—field hockey on the frozen ground, soccer or rugby in rain, mud, snow, or sun, cricket on grass-stained summer afternoons, tennis or track tucked into green evenings. I would have played anything at all if there had been more time, for I took to games well and easily, finding them always pleasurable, conclusive, satisfying. I suppose that the sporting ethos was embedding itself in me all the time, not through any sports master's impulse to instruct or inspire but because the games themselves had built-in rules and attitudes. The games were finite and plentiful, and kept us from ever being bored or having to think beyond them. They

kept us, in fact, from a great deal more; but they remained a separate
world, in which we had some control, and they had the virtue of
never repeating themselves.

*

Schools contrive to make sporting activities as accessible as lunches,
and while we feasted we were also acquiring heroes and preparing
ourselves to be the fans of tomorrow and the tweed-capped sooth-
sayers of fifty years on, for it became obligatory to read about—
and watch, when possible—the muscular stars of the day, to see if
we could add any new twist to our performances or extra manner-
isms to our play. In those years, we knew our sporting statistics
before we knew what statistics were, and would go on sporting pil-
grimages with all the fervor of the faithful. When Scotland played
a rugby match against England, Wales, or Ireland at its voluminous
home ground in Edinburgh, we would be the first to arrive and the
last to leave, wound up in scarves, hoarse, clutching programs for
our private annals, with their photographs of burly, bearded teams
from the past, looking to us as remote in time as Crusaders. We
would marvel at the cleansing effect of passing time. In Britain, a
sharp distinction exists between rugby and soccer, the two principal
winter games. Rugby has traditionally been the elected game of the
"character-building" public schools and the universities, and has re-
mained staunchly amateur, whereas soccer, referred to invariably as
"the working-man's game," went professional early and has always
commanded a huge and pugnacious following in the cities and the
industrial areas. But that is a simplification, for in certain regions—
the mining country of South Wales, and the Scottish Border coun-
try—rugby provokes a religious fervor, and soccer is looked on as
effete by comparison. There is always a hint of class war between
the two codes; but in recent years soccer has come in for—and de-
served—much more attention, for it is *the* universal team game. In
those early days, however, we felt no contradiction, and played both,
with equal zest. Through the agency of an indulgent uncle, I would
get myself taken to soccer games, changing my language and terms
of reference like a bilingual, collecting different programs, adding
to a different vocabulary. And when the turning seasons brought a
different game round, I was ready. The world seemed to be peopled
by nothing more than clusters of teams—a huge sporting pyramid

on some lower step of which we had a hot foothold. Games began and ended; but the Game, we felt, would go on and on and on.

*

The majority of people, I suppose, hang up their sports gear with their school days—all except the conspicuous few who earn a fat living from being watched or who can overcome the inconvenience of keeping their muscles stretched while pursuing another, unsporting life. For the rest, a gradual subsiding moves them from field to terrace, from active to passive. Playing a game brings about moments of zest, of sheer physical pleasure; but these occur to the spectator vicariously, through intense physical empathy. It is almost an inevitable progression—from player to spectator to addict. I am always surprised at how suddenly ex-players turn into sages, as though to become a spectator were the beginning of wisdom. Myself, I still jump at the chance to kick a ball about in any open space, for I have no doubt at all that playing a game is more absorbing in every way than watching one, no matter how miscellaneous the participants or how atrophied the muscles. I have even staged elaborate games of home soccer in the corridors of houses in the middle of cities—games that brought the house down, and that eventually grew elaborate rules. But the weekly spectator must wait for games to happen, and is tied to the time scheme of his vicarious reality—first, a few days of expectation, of calculation, of reading omens, days of scrutinizing the sporting press and watching glimpses of previous games on television, all leading up to Saturday, when the crowds gather, hoping for their expectations to be surpassed, hoping for astonishment, but settling, generally, for a good deal less. Then come the postmortems, the appraisals, as the game shifts from expectation to memory and is tucked away in the record books. The real world is never so reliable. Still, the world of sport keeps offering a steady stream of small unknowns, all to be resolved from week to week. There is enough surprise to keep it interesting, and there is, above all, the satisfaction of a conclusion.

*

As a spectator, I have a long and ubiquitous dedication to games, for I have traveled a lot and shifted countries impulsively, taking whatever sports I have found. I have entered in part into the lives of new places through the sports pages, for they are remarkably alike from one country to another, even in the banality of their sporting metaphors. But the games on show do alter from place to place. Cricket does not raise its languid, well-mannered head in Europe, except in a few unlikely outposts: I once watched on a dusty expanse of ground in the town of Corfu the local Byron Cricket Club play a team from a visiting British frigate—a game unmemorable in every respect but that of its improbable atmosphere. Other countries offer some forms of sport unique to them, which have been handed down carefully from the past. Once, while I was living in the French Basque provinces, I gravitated, with everyone else, on a Saturday in late August to the town of Mauléon-Soule, where the annual Basque Games were being held. It was quite the most cheerful sporting occasion I can remember, helped along by the curious nature of the events. There was a relay race in which the contestants had to run carrying a squirming and squealing piglet to hand on to the next man, and a contest in which the axe-swinging contestants straddled enormous logs and had to chop them in half between their feet. I remember the whole occasion for the great glee shared by spectators and contestants—all the more so now, when sport appears to have lost all trace of humor, if not of pleasure.

*

The crowning sporting occasion, if we are to believe statistics, is the soccer World Cup finals, or the Mundial, as Latin Americans call it, which comes round every four years, and is watched, we are repeatedly told, by over a billion people, or one in five of the world's population. It takes a month to play itself to conclusion, which is a long time to be on the global stage; but it usually manages to come up with enough excitements to overflow the sports pages as well as the screen. It is one sport in which the United States is not a dominant presence—although soccer has tried to squeeze its way into the sporting calendar, it has not managed to lodge itself in the national appetite. The United States, however, does compete in the preliminary competition; and once, during the World Cup finals in Mexico in 1970, watching a game between Italy and Mexico, I heard an announcer say, on my neighbor's transistor, in his most withering tones, "Italy should certainly have scored by now against such feeble opposition as Mexico, who only reached the finals at the expense of such inconsequential countries as Nicaragua and the United States of America." He must have relished the rare opportunity of uttering that sentence.

*

If the British Isles take the cake for the multiplicity of their sporting enthusiasms, Brazil must carry it off for single-mindedness, because in Brazil the national existence is dominated by soccer. Small boys perform prodigious feats with soccer balls in the back streets, and you get the impression that play never stops for a moment. The great heroes of the game, like Pelé, have racked up both fame and fortune from their playing days, in the manner of movie stars, so the small boys keep performing, hoping to be noticed by a stray scout, sure that they, too, can play their way to an otherwise unattainable stardom, and buy houses and cars for their families. The Brazilian soccer crowds are intimidating, so thirsty are they for superhuman performance, so intensely lettered in every twist of the game. But by far the most memorable sporting occasion I witnessed there took place on a damp, deserted Sunday morning in Rio de Janeiro. I went for a walk on the long beach, fairly early, in a light drizzle, with nothing in mind but the morning. On the sand, which through the week belonged to indolent sunbathers and peripatetic kite-fliers, goalposts had taken root, pair after pair, and a string of soccer games was in progress, receding into the far, drizzling distance. Small clumps of watchers stood under colored umbrellas or wandered from game to game, but nobody paid any attention to them—the games were the thing. The players were barefoot, the sand made for heavy going, but the fierce concentration, the inventiveness, and the physical exuberance of the players produced the kind of delighted pleasure that is the real lure of games—the moments of astonishment when players become part of an action that surprises even them. No shouts or whistles, no playing to the crowd, no histrionics, nothing but the game itself. I don't think I have ever seen anywhere else a game played so purely and joyfully for its own sake; and, as far as I was concerned, neither the players nor the teams had names, nor was I likely to watch any of them again. I often think of that morning as an antidote to the puffed-up, overheralded contests that fill the dreary seasons of over-organized sport. I hope the sand games go on and have not been turned into a spectacle.

A friend of mine, a diplomat, was posted to Laos in the fifties. An insatiable soccer fan, he made a point of seeking out local games, where he witnessed this unusual half-time diversion. Here is his account: "When the players left the field for the ten-minute interval, from each goal, a solitary figure emerged. One of the figures wore, covering head and shoulders, a giant penis fashioned out of papier mache and appropriately painted, erect, and pointing forward; the other figure wore, also over head and shoulders, a similarly-fashioned and painted vulva of like dimensions, elliptical and vertical. Neither of the figures could see forward. Through whistles and shouted directions, the crowd attempted to manoeuvre the two figures to within range of one another. At further urging, the vulva opened, and the crowd, now in a state of high excitement, urged the two figures toward one another with such shrill precision that penetration was usually accomplished before the ten minutes had elapsed."

Given the costly and tedious extravaganzas that are staged for our diversion on major sporting occasions, this one has much to be said for it in terms of its economy, its participatory nature, and the clamorous enthusiasm it arouses in the attendant crowd. It may yet take its place among the sporting rituals of our time.

*

The British take sport as something of a national duty; for Spaniards it is pleasure and the excuse for pleasure. They will watch anything with the same delighted disposition, and, equipped with family and friends, they come to sporting occasions in high good humor. I grew used in Spain to seeing babies at bullfights and late-night soccer games, and to being offered a share in the family feasts often unpacked at stadiums. Spaniards are the best-tempered spectators of all; they do not turn ugly, for their insistence on diversion is too great. I once calculated, while I was living in Madrid, that it was physically possible on a Sunday to begin with the illegal cockfights in the morning, take in the soccer match in the early afternoon, scamper to the bullfight, and follow that up with a few choice pelota matches at the *frontón* in the evening. Moreover, sporting occasions in Spain do not have the hearty maleness of those in the British Isles. Women attend with just as much enthusiasm as men, and the occasions are much better for their presence. I relished these Sundays in Madrid, days made for celebration—an exuberant change from the stark and barren Sundays I remembered from Scotland, days of absence and abstinence, where voices scarcely rose above a murmur and games were not played. By the happiest of accidents, I found myself living in the year 1959 at a short sprint from the ground of the Spanish soccer team Real Madrid, then justly the most celebrated team in the world, and I made a habit of watching the players every time they filled their famous oval stadium. I had never seen the game of soccer played with such cool mastery, such panache and skill, and I could look forward to these games with schoolboy keenness, sure of seeing something pulled out of the hat. From the soccer point of view, it was like living at the center of the world. What was most curious in the Spain of those days was the huge switch in Spaniards' allegiance from the bullfight to soccer. Various scandals had discredited the bullfight across the years, even though it was still felt to be more ritual than sport. For a few seasons, I had the *afición*, as Spaniards say—the passion. But the more one learns of the intricacies of the bullfight, the more one becomes aware of the pretenses and deceptions practiced by matadors. In any case, tourists could then be counted on to fill the bullrings, for the sake of the experience. So even staunch Spanish aficionados were deserting the bullring in droves for the football stadium, angry at the tourist-pleasing travesties of the classic corrida. The controversy raged in the press and in the cafés, but I suspect that a great many Spaniards, for all their vehemence, kept on attending both, with their habitual delight.

*

Probably the worst sporting summer I have ever spent was one in France, when I lived in an old water mill in the Pyrenees. Nothing at all showed up on the sports pages of the regional newspaper, the *Sud-Ouest*, save the impending Tour de France, the enormous bicycling cavalcade that keeps the French in a running lather throughout the month of July. Bicycles I love, as single objects, but bicycle racing, with its intricate team strategies and on such a scale, seemed altogether beyond my capacity for enthusiasm. Still, there was nothing else, and when I discovered that one of the *étapes* of the Tour was due to pass through a town some thirty kilometers away I could not resist going there. It proved to be the most disappointing event of my sporting life. I went there early in the day, took in my share of anticipatory atmospherics, settled myself in the makeshift stands well in advance—hours in advance—waited, read, dozed, talked with my neighbors, and was rewarded for all that laborious anticipation with some six minutes of hysterical whoosh as seventy-odd cyclists flashed past at a speed too fast for the eye to follow, bracketed by a tedious parade of publicity on wheels. I think it was the only time my spectating zeal deserted me entirely, for I gave up reading the newspapers after that, and never bothered to find out who won the whole grueling pilgrimage.

*

The transition from player to spectator is, I suppose, one that the passing of time makes inevitable, although I would still rather play anything, even if it has to be table tennis or croquet, than surrender totally to spectatorhood; nor do I want knowing *about* games to replace the games themselves. Of course, in our time television does our watching for us, and has reduced spectating to a state of passivity approaching mindlessness. British television covers sporting events as though they were moon shots, assembling panels of experts days before games are due to take place—a procedure that the TV people refer to as their buildup. Experts do our speculating for us—something that annoys me intensely—and their painful prognostications are interspersed with clips of games going back into sporting antiquity, possibly to give us a proper sense of the sporting past. I prefer the old men in bars any day. The play itself is heavy with commentary, so that it has become impossible to watch for oneself, to watch without being told what one is seeing. Commentators have, or feel they have, an obligation to inject excitement into the proceedings, and tend to smother the action in exclamatory superlatives. But television has devised an even more ingenious way of tampering with perception, even with time itself, through the device of instant replay. No sooner has some crucial incident taken place than there it is, happening all over again, not once but several times—in slow motion, from a variety of angles; and if it should be a decisive goal we are bound to see it half a dozen times more during the postmortems. It may well go into the annals, to be replayed next year, next decade, whenever the same sporting occasion next takes place. Instant replay makes memory seem humbling by comparison, yet memory is all we have and, I tend to feel, all we need to have, or ought to have. I look back to a time when games happened once and then passed happily into oblivion. Soon we will be crying out for instant replay as part of our everyday perception. Soon we may give up the hazard of slogging to stadiums altogether, and choose instead either to watch games from the sporting past played over and over or to see, possibly before long, others, specially put together for television—games that never really happen at all.

*

Have sports improved or declined with time? This question gets a voluminous going over from sportswriters and pundits, who mostly point out the great strides made and the enormous present-day public involvement. Yet when I cast my mind back, and when I see film clips of ancient encounters, it occurs to me that perhaps only the technology and the organization have evolved—the clips appear fast and jerky, the uniforms clumsy, the haircuts at odds with ours. The play itself is no less exuberant, however, nor are the crowds any less enthusiastic; and most of the old men I know sturdily insist that the players of the past were far more individually inventive than the overtrained robots of today. Certainly in my own past there were teams and occasions that thrilled me far more than anything in the present—but the argument is an impossible one. We have the same difficulty in, say, appreciating the beauty of women from yellowing photographs that we have in tuning in to the skill or excitement of faded, jerky rugby games. Rules have been streamlined somewhat. Records have been improved on, indisputably—but progress in sport has more to do with technological and physiological advance, and with fashion, than with anything else. Most probably, we all have a point in our lives at which sporting events involve and excite us to a degree that is never repeated, so that the games themselves appear to some to decline and to others to improve. Unquestionably, sports are now approached in such a ruthlessly systematic way that the heroes of the past seem no more than happy-go-lucky adventurers. I'm not sure I don't prefer them, in their flapping uniforms and huge boots, but, then, sports age in a way peculiar to themselves. It surprises me that we have stuck so closely to the canon of established sports, and have not invented a whole slew of new games, unencumbered by record books. It might help us to take the entire sporting effort less grimly, to get back to the principles of pleasure and play.

*

In March of 1975, the London *Sunday Times* published a collection of the opinions of a variety of sportswriters on the ills of sport. It surprised me to read the wistful plaints and discerning grouses, for sportswriters generally give the impression of living comfortably in their separate sporting reality, and write of games with the gravity and high seriousness of war correspondents. On this occasion, some of them took the spectators' part, and castigated various sports in turn for failing to entertain, for succumbing to negative tactics, for bending the rules, for regimenting individual eccentricity. Those who wrote from the players' side complained of pressures and programs that turned the game sour, killing pleasure and weakening commitment. Obviously, all is not well in sporting circles, and for a whole anthology of reasons. Keith Botsford, in a perceptive short piece, saw sport in its proper perspective, as part of present-day society— as a consequence of it. The mixing of sport and money, he noted, had led to the exploitation of both players and public. Sport as pure activity or game had long since given way to ruthless organization. And he added:

A lot is due to the way in which the body has become one of the cardinal concepts of twentieth-century life. Pandered to by armies of equipment-makers, pros, sexologists, dieticians, doctors, ministries abetted by promoters and over-eager hockey mistresses alike, the sports body has reached the obsessive stage and lost sight of its original intention of pleasure.

It seems ironic that the well-legislated activities that the British planted magnanimously in so many unlikely foreign contexts have turned into major social confusions. What was clear was that nobody mixed up in sport, either on or off the field, was having much fun. It all confirmed me in an opinion I have had for some time: that the sporting context is ripe for anthropologists; that when they are ranging around for a proper context in which to do fieldwork, they ought to converge on the sports field. There is nothing simple about the problems that beset organized sport, nothing that can be corrected by changing the rules or the shape of the ball; but it is at least an area over which we can legislate fairly directly, a subreality that we ought to be able to modify quite drastically. Sport is not a matter of life and death, but it appears to be doing little more at the moment than defeating its own purpose.

*

The point about games is that they came into being—and keep on coming into being—to pass the time. Pastimes, *passe-temps*. The imperceptible flow of time is intolerable without some punctuation, and games are precisely that. Their rules impose a brief order, and we enter into them for as long as they last. But they are not meant to have a separate, tyrannical existence. It is not surprising that the English have been responsible for launching so many games, because they have a strongly compulsive bent toward order. But one has to be wary of being carried away by the neat orderliness of a game, for it is to some extent a deception. The larger confusion has arisen as games have continued through time and acquired a lore and a past, as sport has developed into a vast, worldwide enterprise. It is from this that I feel we ought to dissociate ourselves, because games imply activity, not passivity—the activity of a player, not the passivity of a spectator. If games are meant to be a temporary, passing pleasure, as I think they are, then surely, in an existential sense, we ought to forget them the moment they are over. They are there to be played again and again. Any attempt to keep them happening in language or on film seems superfluous, and irrelevant to their purpose. The moment, the act of playing, the pleasure of their happening—these are what count. But games serve different purposes for different people. I recall a friend of mine, a passionate soccer follower, saying to me some years ago, "I once contemplated suicide; and then I thought, How could I bear not knowing whether Chelsea would win or not next Saturday, and every Saturday after that? So I put the thought out of my head."

*

The relevance of Borges' story to the sporting scene has never been more clearly demonstrated than in the occasional confrontations, increasing over the last few years, between political realists and the ruling authorities in the world of sport. If the British used to treat war as though it were a game of cricket, international matches, especially on the soccer field, are now likely to be viewed as war—if not by the players, then, most bluntly, by the fans. I doubt very much whether sport can any longer be maintained as a separate, innocent reality. Sporting events have become real events, not play; and as such they are subject to all the confusions of our tangled reality.

*

I look with some awe on those who have managed to avoid the ranging tentacles of sport, although their numbers must surely have shrunk through the agency of television, which in England claims to have converted legions of housewives to manly pursuits. It seems that only lighthouse keepers are invulnerable. It is certainly diffi- cult to remain aloof from the attendant hoo-ha—notably from the legions of fans who trudge in the wake of their teams, especially soccer fans, whose antics constitute a national menace in Britain. A soccer game lasts only ninety minutes, but the pilgrimage under- taken by the visiting fans may well last the whole weekend, leaving a considerable amount of loose time. Of late, the fans have taken to filling this time by dismantling trains, buses, stores, bars, and rival fans, and in retrospect the season's casualty list looks brutal. In May of 1975, Scotland's soccer team was due to play England at Wembley Stadium, on the outskirts of London, and while much of the country quivered in anticipation a good proportion of London's population quivered for quite other reasons. Scotland was favored to win on form, but every contest between these two ancient ene- mies invokes a bloodstained history of resentment, given more of an edge by the recent upsurge of nationalism in Scotland. The suburban train drivers who run the service from the city center to the stadium announced a Saturday strike in protest over the last thunderous visit of the Scottish fans—a rampage that had brought serious injury to one railwayman. This left the majority of the fans with an eight-mile walk out to the stadium, and shopkeepers along the route took to boarding up their windows. By Friday evening, London looked as though it had been invaded—knots of Scotsmen splashed the city with tartan scarves and bonnets, and their flags wagged on the street corners. The bars were thick with dire, guttural prognostications. On Saturday morning, I felt I had never seen so many of my country- men, even in Scotland, for they were already singing victory songs, and seemed ready to take over the seat of government if Scotland won. That morning, I was passing through the park close to where I live when I ran into a neighbor, a retired naval man, who stopped me. "It is not my wont to watch football matches," he said gravely, "but I intend to follow this afternoon's proceedings closely. I have calculated, from experience, that if Scotland should lose, which appears unlikely, then its followers will behave in a subdued manner, and be reduced to morbid introspection. But should it win, then I fear for the safety of our persons and our institutions. Is this not a situation which alarms you?" It was, I said; and it did. I watched the game anxiously, and, improbably, England hit form and won, by five emphatic goals to one. The old man was right—the fans were subdued, and London survived. And, may my ancestors forgive me, I was relieved.

TRANSLATION

Translation is a mysterious alchemy. To recreate work written in one language in the trappings of another is always a hazardous undertaking, and demands from the translator not just a deep reading of the original but all the insight and ingenuity he can summon up in his own language. As Borges himself put it: "Nothing is as consubstantial with literature and its modest mystery as the questions raised by a translation."

What Gets Lost/Lo Que Se Pierde

I keep translating *traduzco continuamente*
entre palabras words *que no son las mias*
into other words which are mine *de palabras a mis palabras.*
Y finalmente de quien es el texto?
Who do words belong to?
Del escritor o del traductor writer, translator
o de los idiomas or to language itself?
Traductores, somos fantasmas que viven
entre aquel mundo y el nuestro
translators are ghosts who live
in a limbo between two worlds
pero poco a poco me ocurre
que el problema no es cuestion
de lo que se pierde en traducion
the problem is not a question
of what gets lost in translation
sino but rather *lo que se pierde*
what gets lost
entre la ocurrencia—sea de amor o de agonia
between the happening of love or pain
y el hecho de que llega
a existir en palabras
and their coming into words.

Para nosotros todos, amantes, habladores
for lovers or users of words
el problema es este this is the difficulty—
lo que se pierde what gets lost
no es lo que se pierde en traducion sino
is not what gets lost in translation but more
what gets lost in language itself *lo que se pierde*
en el hecho en la lengua,
en la palabra misma.

Translator to Poet

For Pablo Neruda, 1904–1973

There are only the words left now. They lie like tombstones
or the stone Andes where the green scrub ends.
I do not have the heart to chip away
at your long lists of joy, which alternate
their iron and velvet, all the vegetation
and whalebone of your chosen stormy coast.
So much was written hope, with every line
extending life by saying, every meeting
ending in expectation of the next.
It was your slow intoning voice which counted,
bringing a living Chile into being
where poetry was bread, where books were banquets.
Now they are silent, stony on the shelf.
I cannot read them for the thunderous silence,
the grief of Chile's dying and your own,
death being the one definitive translation.

The Great Tablecloth

When they were called to the table,
the tyrants came rushing
with their temporary ladies,
it was fine to watch the women pass
like wasps with big bosoms
followed by those pale
and unfortunate public tigers.

The peasant in the field ate
his poor quota of bread,
he was alone, it was late,
he was surrounded by wheat,
but he had no more bread;
he ate it with grim teeth,
looking at it with hard eyes.

In the blue hour of eating,
the infinite hour of the roast,
the poet abandons his lyre,
takes up his knife and fork,
puts his glass on the table,
and the fishermen attend
the little sea of the soup bowl.
Burning potatoes protest
among the tongues of oil.
The lamb is gold on its coals
and the onion undresses.
It is sad to eat in dinner clothes,
like eating in a coffin,
but eating in convents
is like eating underground.
Eating alone is a disappointment,
but not eating matters more,
is hollow and green, has thorns
like a chain of fish-hooks
trailing from the heart,
clawing at your insides.

Hunger feels like pincers,
like the bite of crabs,
it burns, burns and has no fire.
Hunger is a cold fire.
Let us sit down soon to eat
with all those who haven't eaten;
let us spread great tablecloths,
put salt in the lakes of the world,
set up planetary bakeries,
tables with strawberries in snow,
and a plate like the moon itself
from which we can all eat.

For now I ask no more
than the justice of eating.

                                    Pablo Neruda

How Much Happens in a Day

In the course of a day we shall meet one another.

But, in one day, things spring to life—
they sell grapes in the street,
tomatoes change their skin,
the young girl you wanted
never came back to the office.

They changed the postman suddenly.
The letters now are not the same.
A few golden leaves, and it's different;
this tree is now well-off.

Who would have said that the earth
with its ancient skin would change so much?
It has more volcanoes than yesterday,
the sky has brand-new clouds,
the rivers are flowing differently.
Besides, so much has come into being!

I have inaugurated hundreds
of highways and buildings,
delicate, clean bridges
like ships or violins.

And so, when I greet you
and kiss your flowering mouth,
our kisses are other kisses,
our mouths are other mouths.

Joy, my love, joy in all things,
in what falls and what flourishes.

Joy in today and yesterday,
the day before and tomorrow.

Joy in bread and stone,
joy in fire and rain.

In what changes, is born, grows,
consumes itself, and becomes a kiss again.

Joy in the air we have,
and in what we have of earth.

When our life dries up,
only the roots remain to us,
and the wind is cold like hate.

Then let us change our skin,
our nails, our blood, our gazing,
and you kiss me and I go out
to sell light on the roads.

Joy in the night and the day,
and the four stations of the soul.

Pablo Neruda

Emerging

A man says yes without knowing
how to decide even what the question is,
and is caught up, and then is carried along
and never again escapes from his own cocoon;
and that's how we are, forever falling
into the deep well of other beings;
and one thread wraps itself around our necks,
another entwines a foot, and then it is impossible,
impossible to move except in the well—
nobody can rescue us from other people.

It seems as if we don't know how to speak;
it seems as if there are words which escape,
which are missing, which have gone away and left us
to ourselves, tangled up in snares and threads.

And all at once, that's it; we no longer know
what it's all about, but we are deep inside it,
and now we will never see with the same eyes
as once we did when we were children playing.
Now these eyes are closed to us,
now our hands emerge from different arms.

And therefore, when you sleep, you are alone in your dreaming,
and running freely through the corridors
of one dream only, which belongs to you.
Oh never let them come to steal our dreams,
never let them entwine us in our bed.
Let us hold on to the shadows
to see if, from our own obscurity,
we emerge and grope along the walls,
lie in wait for the light, to capture it,
till, once and for all time,
it becomes our own, the sun of every day.

Pablo Neruda

Where Can Guillermina Be?

Where can Guillermina be?

When my sister invited her
and I went out to open the door,
the sun came in, the stars came in,
two tresses of wheat came in
and two inexhaustible eyes.

I was fourteen years old,
brooding, and proud of it,
slim, lithe and frowning,
funereal and formal.
I lived among the spiders,
dank from the forest,
the beetles knew me,
and the three-coloured bees.
I slept among partridges,
hidden under the mint.

Then Guillermina entered
with her blue lightning eyes
which swept across my hair
and pinned me like swords
against the wall of winter.
That happened in Temuco,
there in the South, on the frontier.

The years have passed slowly,
pacing like pachiderms,
barking like crazy foxes.
The soiled years have passed,
waxing, worn, funereal,
and I walked from cloud to cloud,
from land to land, from eye to eye,
while the rain on the frontier
fell in its same grey shape.

My heart has travelled
in the same faithful shoes,
and I have endured the thorns.
I had no rest where I was:
where I hit out, I was struck,
where they murdered me I fell;
and I revived, as fresh as ever,
and then and then and then and then—
it all takes so long to tell.

I have nothing to add.

I came to live in this world.

Where can Guillermina be?

Pablo Neruda

Lazybones

They will continue wandering,
these things of steel among the stars,
and worn-out men will still go up
to brutalize the placid moon.
There, they will found their pharmacies.

In this time of the swollen grape,
the wine begins to come to life
between the sea and the mountain ranges.

In Chile now, cherries are dancing,
the dark, secretive girls are singing,
and in guitars, water is shining.

The sun is touching every door
and making wonder of the wheat.

The first wine is pink in colour,
is sweet with the sweetness of a child,
the second wine is able-bodied,
strong like the voice of a sailor,
the third wine is a topaz, is
a poppy and a fire in one.

My house has both the sea and the earth,
my woman has great eyes
the colour of wild hazelnut,
when night comes down, the sea
puts on a dress of white and green,
and later the moon in the spindrift foam
dreams like a sea-green girl.

I have no wish to change my planet.

Pablo Neruda

On the Death of Borges

W H E N T H E N E W S reached us of the death, at eighty-six, of Jorge Luis Borges, in Geneva, on June 14, 1986, it brought not just the pang we felt at the loss of his wise, beguiling presence but also the peculiar shiver of disquiet that his writings often generate. In our issue of June 2, we published a poem of his, in which he speculates on his death. It begins:

> Which of my cities
> am I doomed to die in?
> Geneva,
> where revelation reached me
> from Virgil and Tacitus
> (certainly not from Calvin)?

In retrospect, the poem's appearance has about it that very shiver of coincidence which we have come to call Borgesian, after the Master—for we have found that reading certain of his stories and poems has the effect of casting quite ordinary happenings in a strange, vertiginous light. One of Borges' chosen Spanish words was *asombro*, which means "astonishment," or, better, "awe." Awe was what Borges found at the heart of great literature; awe was what he felt about the myriad chance crossings in human existence—"the webbed scheme," as he called it—and awe was what, through his quirky essays, his disturbing fictions, his fantastic stories, and his meditative poems, he aroused in his readers. In a famous essay of his, "Kafka and His Precursors," he demonstrates how after we have read the world through Kafka's eyes we find his influence even in writers who came before him in time. So it is with Borges: once we have read him, we sense his curious presence everywhere—in the past, in chance happenings, in the context of our own lives.

More than any other writer, Borges lived in and through literature. For him, reading was a form of time travel; his favorite writers were his friends; and, before his blindness finally descended, he had learned a whole library by heart. From a very early age, he had understood that it was his destiny to be a writer; and, indeed, no one has done more honor to that solitary office. Yet Borges never failed to point out the ironies implicit in making written sense of the world: a book, once written, mocks the writer by outlasting him, and the eternities created by the imagination are rendered ironic by the inevitability of death. Even so, for Borges it was only in writing that the living moment could be held, saved from oblivion; and literature, the sum of those written moments, was, for him, consolation enough. Just as literature had given him life, he turned his life into literature—literature of a spare and wondrous variety—and the facts of his life, such as his blindness, became metaphors in his writing. "When writers die," he once said, "they become books, which is, after all, not too bad an incarnation."

It is not every writer who adds to his work by his presence; but as Borges' writings infiltrated other languages he was much sought after, and late in his life he grew prodigal with his time, traveling to different countries, giving many lectures and interviews, appearing on international television, and answering endless questions with unfailing courtesy. At one time, his readers felt themselves to be members of a secret society; now they are legion. Many who had read him came to hear him, and carried away, as a talisman, an image of him that added affection to awe: frail, soft-spoken in both English and Spanish, his hands clasping a walking stick in front of him, he mesmerized his listeners with his careful phrasing, his modesty, his wit, the warm and often mischievous humor of his spoken asides. We recall a conversation we had with him just over a year ago, in which he talked about his traveling; he referred to it, characteristically, as "seeing the world." "When I am at home in Buenos Aires," he told us, "one day is much like another. But when I travel—and you must realize that for me, since I am blind, traveling means merely changing armchairs—friendly ghosts materialize one by one and talk to me about literature, and about my own works, most generously. For a writer, that is great luxury. I feel blessed by it, I feel lucky." Besides his books, his gentle ghost is very much with us.

Matthew XXV: 30

The first bridge, Constitution Station. At my feet
the shunting trains trace iron labyrinths.
Steam hisses up and up into the night,
which becomes at a stroke the night of the Last Judgment.

From the unseen horizon
and from the very center of my being,
an infinite voice pronounced these things—
things, not words. This is my feeble translation,
time-bound, of what was a single limitless Word:

"Stars, bread, libraries of East and West,
playing-cards, chessboards, galleries, skylights, cellars,
a human body to walk with on the earth,
fingernails, growing at night-time and in death,
shadows for forgetting, mirrors busily multiplying,
cascades in music, gentlest of all time's shapes.
Borders of Brazil, Uruguay, horses and mornings,
a bronze weight, a copy of the Grettir Saga,
algebra and fire, the charge at Junin in your blood,
days more crowded than Balzac, scent of the honeysuckle,
love and the imminence of love and intolerable remembering,
dreams like buried treasure, generous luck,
and memory itself, where a glance can make men dizzy—
all this was given to you, and with it
the ancient nourishment of heroes—
treachery, defeat, humiliation.
In vain have oceans been squandered on you, in vain
the sun, wonderfully seen through Whitman's eyes.
You have used up the years and they have used up you,
and still, and still, you have not written the poem."

Jorge Luis Borges

The Other Tiger

And the craft createth a semblance.
—MORRIS, *Sigurd the Volsung* (1876)

I think of a tiger. The half-light enhances
the vast and painstaking library
and seems to set the bookshelves at a distance;
strong, innocent, bloodstained, and new-made,
it will move through its jungle and its morning,
and leave its track across the muddy
edge of a river, unknown, nameless
(in its world, there are no names, nor past, nor future—
only the sureness of the passing moment)
and it will cross the wilderness of distance
and sniff out in the woven labyrinth
of smells the smell peculiar to morning
and the scent of deer, delectable.
Among the slivers of bamboo, I notice
its stripes, and I have an inkling of the skeleton
under the magnificence of the skin, which quivers.
In vain, the convex oceans and the deserts
spread themselves across the earth between us;
from this one house in a remote lost seaport
in South America, I dream you, follow you,
oh tiger on the fringes of the Ganges.

Afternoon creeps in my spirit and I keep thinking
that the tiger I am conjuring in my poem
is a tiger made of symbols and of shadows,
a sequence of prosodic measures,
scraps remembered from encyclopedias,
and not the deadly tiger, the luckless jewel
which in the sun or the deceptive moonlight
follows its paths, in Bengal or Sumatra,
of love, of indolence, of dying.
Against the symbolic tiger, I have put
the real one, whose blood runs hot,

234

and today, 1959, the third of August,
a slow shadow spreads across the prairie,
but still, the act of naming it, of guessing
what is its nature and its circumstances
creates a fiction, not a living creature,
not one of those who wander on the earth.

Let us look for a third tiger. This one
will be a form in my dream like all the others,
a system and arrangement of human language,
and not the flesh-and-bone tiger
which, out of reach of all mythology,
paces the earth. I know all this, but something
drives me to this ancient and vague adventure,
unreasonable, and still I keep on looking
throughout the afternoon for the other tiger,
the other tiger which is not in this poem.

Jorge Luis Borges

Limits

Of all the streets that blur into the sunset,
there must be one (which, I am not sure)
that I by now have walked for the last time
without guessing it, the pawn of that Someone

who fixes in advance omnipotent laws,
sets up a secret and unwavering scale
for all the shadows, dreams, and forms
woven into the texture of this life.

If there is a limit to all things and a measure
and a last time and nothing more and forgetfulness,
who will tell us to whom in this house
we without knowing it have said farewell?

Through the dawning window night withdraws
and among the stacked books which throw
irregular shadows on the dim table,
there must be one which I will never read.

There is in the South more than one worn gate,
with its cement urns and planted cactus,
which is already forbidden to my entry,
inaccessible, as in a lithograph.

There is a door you have closed for ever
and some mirror is expecting you in vain;
to you the crossroads seem wide open,
yet watching you, four-faced, is a Janus.

There is among all your memories one
which has now been lost beyond recall.
You will not be seen going down to that fountain,
neither by white sun nor by yellow moon.

You will never recapture what the Persian
said in his language woven with birds and roses,

when, in the sunset, before the light disperses,
you wish to give words to unforgettable things.

And the steadily-flowing Rhone and the lake,
all that vast yesterday over which today I bend?
They will be as lost as Carthage,
scourged by the Romans with fire and salt.

At dawn I seem to hear the turbulent
murmur of crowds milling and fading away;
they are all I have been loved by, forgotten by;
space, time, and Borges now are leaving me.

Jorge Luis Borges

Rain

Quite suddenly the evening clears at last
as now outside the soft small rain is falling.
Falling or fallen. Rain itself is something
undoubtedly which happens in the past.

Whoever hears it falling has remembered
a time in which a curious twist of fate
brought back to him a flower whose name was "rose"
and the perplexing redness of its red.

This rain which spreads its blind across the pane
must also brighten in forgotten suburbs
the black grapes on a vine across a shrouded

patio now no more. The evening's rain
brings me the voice, the dear voice of my father,
who comes back now, who never has been dead.

Jorge Luis Borges

The Web

Which of my cities
am I doomed to die in?
Geneva,
where revelation reached me
from Virgil and Tacitus
(certainly not from Calvin)?
Montevideo,
where Luis Melián Lafinur,
blind and heavy with years,
died among the archives
of that impartial
history of Uruguay
he never wrote?
Nara,
where in a Japanese inn
I slept on the floor
and dreamed the terrible
image of the Buddha
I had touched without seeing
but saw in my dream?
Buenos Aires,
where I verge on being a foreigner?
Austin, Texas,
where my mother and I
in the autumn of '61
discovered America?
What language
am I doomed to die in?
The Spanish my ancestors used
to call for the charge, or to play *truco*?
The English of the Bible
my grandmother read from
at the edges of the desert?
What time will it happen?
In the dove-colored twilight
when color drains away,
or in the twilight of the crow

when night abstracts and simplifies
all visible things?
Or at an inconsequential moment—
two in the afternoon?
These questions are
digressions that stem not from fear
but from impatient hope.
They form part of the fateful web
of cause and effect
that no man can foresee,
nor any god.

Jorge Luis Borges

Afterword

OF TRANSLATION, Octavio Paz once wrote: "In writing an original poem we are translating the world, transmuting it. Everything we do is translation, and all translations are in a way creations. The poet is the universal translator." I think this is true about the act of writing, be it poetry or prose. It is all a matter of translating wordless perceptions and insights into language, into words that will appropriately contain them. There is no clear point of arrival, no definitive version. There is only the endless business of looking for the right words and, sometimes, being lucky enough to find them.

Acknowledgments

A good part of the material in this collection has been reprinted from *Weathering: Poems and Translation* and *Whereabouts: Notes on Being a Foreigner*. Other material has been taken from *Ounce Dice Trice*, and from various volumes of translation. Much of the contents originally appeared in *The New Yorker*.

ESSAYS

"Digging up Scotland," "Other People's Houses," "Basilisks' Eggs," and "In Memoriam, Amada" reprinted from *Whereabouts: Notes on Being a Foreigner*, copyright © 1987 by Alastair Reid.
"Waiting for Columbus" first appeared in *The New Yorker*, 24 February 1992.
"Heavy Breathing" first appeared, under the title "Heavy Going," in *The New Yorker*, 21 February 1977.
"On the Death of Borges" first appeared in "The Talk of the Town" in *The New Yorker*, 7 July 1986.

BOOK REVIEWS

The book reviews originally appeared in *The New Yorker*.

POEMS

"The Web" first appeared in *The New Yorker*.
The other poems in this book (excluding "Poem Without Ends" and "Where Truth Lies") appeared earlier in *Weathering: Poems and Translations*, copyright © 1987 by Alastair Reid.

UNIVERSITY PRESS OF NEW ENGLAND publishes books under its own imprint and is the publisher for Brandeis University Press, Brown University Press, University of Connecticut, Dartmouth College, Middlebury College Press, University of New Hampshire, University of Rhode Island, Tufts University, University of Vermont, Wesleyan University Press, and Salzburg Seminar.

LIBRARY OF CONGRESS CATALOGING-IN-PUBLICATION DATA

Reid, Alastair, 1926–
    [Selections]
    An Alastair Reid reader : selected prose and poetry.
        p.   cm. — (Bread Loaf series of contemporary writers)
    ISBN 0–87451–692–7. — ISBN 0–87451–693–5 (pbk.)
    I. Title.   II. series.
PR6035.E4A6   1994
828'.91409—dc20   94–20521
∞